Ferdinand von Mueller

Description and Illustrations of the Myoporinous Plants of Australia

Vol. 2. Lithograms

Ferdinand von Mueller

Description and Illustrations of the Myoporinous Plants of Australia
Vol. 2. Lithograms

ISBN/EAN: 9783337315153

Printed in Europe, USA, Canada, Australia, Japan

Cover: Foto ©Andreas Hilbeck / pixelio.de

More available books at **www.hansebooks.com**

DESCRIPTION AND ILLUSTRATIONS

OF THE

MYOPORINOUS PLANTS OF AUSTRALIA,

BY

BARON FERD. VON MUELLER, K.C.M.G., M.D., PH.D., F.R.S.,

GOVERNMENT BOTANIST FOR VICTORIA.

II.

LITHOGRAMS.

"Dominus solificavit diesfungue aridos quasi bonum aquae delicias."— *Prophetia Isaiae*, li. 3.

BY AUTHORITY:
JOHN FERRES, GOVERNMENT PRINTER, MELBOURNE.
1886.

TO

THE HONORABLE JAMES SERVICE,

𝔏ate 𝔓remier of the Colony of Victoria,

THIS WORK

IS DEDICATED IN RECOGNITION OF GENEROUS SUPPORT,

ACCORDED THROUGH MANY YEARS TO VICTORIAN SCIENTIFIC PURSUITS,

AND IN APPRECIATION OF

CIRCUMSPECT EFFORTS FOR THE ADVANCEMENT OF

THE INTERESTS OF ALL AUSTRALIA.

PREFACE.

Among more extensive orders of plants in the vegetation of the globe four are almost exclusively Australian, namely Candolleaceæ, Goodeniaceæ, Epacrideæ and Myoporinæ; they therefore can find their fullest systematic elucidation also best in our part of the world. The last mentioned ordinal group is the only one of these four, which consists of frutescent and arborescent plants entirely, and which on this account forms at many places a prominent part in the Australian Flora. It is also this order, which is more extensively distributed over all parts of the Australian Continent, than the three other large and nearly endemic ordinal groups above mentioned, the Myoporinæ indeed attaining their highest development in the hottest and most arid regions of this portion of the globe. Moreover it is the object of the present volume, to place on permanent record these beautiful and remarkable plants, before any of them succumbs to impending utter annihilation through close depasturing of runs or through methodic burning of the scrubs, to which the native vegetation becomes more and more subjected. The delineations now offered are all from the hand of Herr R. Graff; they do credit to his artistic skill, and this all the more, as these lithographic drawings are his first effort in botanic direction. Thus now all the 74 hitherto known Australian Myoporinæ have become illustrated on as many plates, each of the latter representing a well-defined species. Gladly would I have given colored pictures of these plants, could this have been possible within the means available; but by extending the illustrative work to chromo-lithography or to hand-coloring, the expenditure of issue and therewith the price of the work would have become doubled or trebled. The descriptive portion of this publication will be given somewhat later; and this for the present will be less missed, as in Bentham's flora Australiensis all former writings on this order including the full synonyms have been collected and systematically re-arranged, so far as the species were known till 1870, while furthermore descriptive elucidations of Myoporinæ are accessible through the eleven volumes of the fragmenta phytographiæ Australiæ, commenced in 1858 and carried on till recent times. Of any medicinal or economic or technologic value, perhaps to be assigned to the numerous species of this order, very little is known beyond the fact, that pastural animals are readily browsing on the foliage of some of the species; but the time has come, when with augmented appliances here these plants can be submitted to exact therapeutic and industrial tests, for which through the pages of the present work a solid basis is gained. A hope is also entertained, that through information, conveyed by this volume, many more of the really gay Myoporinous plants will become early added to garden-shrubberies in milder zones

PREFACE.

and to the conservatory-plants in colder countries, especially as the time of flowering of many Myoporinæ extends over several if not all months of the year;—the frequent failure of raising these handsome shrubs resulting in many cases from not liberating the small seeds by mechanical removal of the hard and often ample pericarp, a process which in nature is not rarely accelerated or facilitated by bush-fires, or by the digestive organs of the emu, or by a kind of spontaneous forcing in the native soil. As regards the gradual discovery of these often far-hidden plants it may aptly here be observed, that the first three members of the order were brought to scientific notice through Cook's expeditions by Banks and Solander and by R. and G. Forster from New Zealand and New Caledonia. Sixteen were added in 1810 by R. Brown during Flinders' voyage, all from Australia, but then also the Antillan Bontia became settled in this group; by these means the order of Myoporinæ was also at the time separately established. Alphonse de Candolle in elaborating the myoporinous plants for the 11th volume of the prodromus systematis naturalis regni vegetabilis mustered 28 genuine species in 1847, from various sources, as all then known, four of the additional plants being from China, Japan, Hawaia and Rodriguez respectively. Bentham in 1870 recorded 59 species, 28 exclusively from our collections here. Since then almost solely through Melbourne-researches the order has numerically been advanced to 74 well limited specific forms for Australia, all here illustrated; thus, if the anomalous South-African Oftia or Spielmannia becomes excluded, this ordinal group of plants counts now a total of 80 species. It is and will be of interest—particularly so for phyto-geographic studies—to watch, whether this order will yet be found represented in any hitherto unexplored region of the globe, perhaps such as New Guinea or Madagascar; but it is not likely, to furnish additions from any highlands, as none of the Australian species proved alpine. But even here we have yet certainly much to learn, concerning the geographic distribution of the known specific kinds over the Australian Continent; and any help also in this particular respect by transmissions of material from far-inland tracts of country will in the interest of science be gratefully welcomed.

Melbourne, May 1886.

ALPHABETIC INDEX.

Name	Plate
Eremophila adenotricha, F. v. M.	53
E. alternifolia, R. Brown	32
E. Behriana, F. v. M.	44
E. bignoniflora, F. v. M.	15
E. Bowmani, F. v. M.	18
E. brevifolia, F. v. M.	45
E. Brownii, F. v. M.	38
E. Clarkei, F. v. M.	30
E. crassifolia, F. v. M.	46
E. Dalyana, F. v. M.	41
E. Delisseri, F. v. M.	43
E. Dempsteri, F. v. M.	51
E. densifolia, F. v. M.	49
E. denticulata, F. v. M.	34
E. divaricata, F. v. M.	55
E. Drummondi, F. v. M.	5
E. Duttoni, F. v. M.	36
E. Elderi, F. v. M.	7
E. eriocalyx, F. v. M.	17
E. exilifolia, F. v. M.	28
E. Forresti, F. v. M.	20
E. Fraseri, F. v. M.	8
E. Freelingi, F. v. M.	11
E. gibbosifolia, F. v. M.	52
E. Gibsoni, F. v. M.	29
E. Gilesii, F. v. M.	4
E. Goodwini, F. v. M.	2
E. graciliflora, F. v. M.	12
E. Hughesii, F. v. M.	3
E. Lanaii, F. v. M.	14
E. latifolia, F. v. M.	33
E. Latrobei, F. v. M.	31
E. leucophylla, Bentham	21
E. longifolia, F. v. M.	13
E. Macdonnelli, F. v. M.	1
E. Mackinlayi, F. v. M.	22
E. maculata, F. v. M.	35

Name	Plate
Eremophila Maitlandi, F. v. M.	19
E. microtheca, F. v. M.	48
E. Mitchelli, Bentham	25
E. Oldfieldi, F. v. M.	37
E. oppositifolia, R. Brown	24
E. Paisleyi, F. v. M.	26
E. Pantoni, F. v. M.	42
E. platycalyx, F. v. M.	10
E. polyclada, F. v. M.	16
E. resinosa, F. v. M.	Supplement 2
E. rotundifolia, F. v. M.	9
E. santalina, F. v. M.	54
E. scoparia, F. v. M.	40
E. strongylophylla, F. v. M.	23
E. Sturtii, R. Brown	27
E. viscida, Endlicher	Supplement 1
E. Weldii, F. v. M.	50
E. Willsii, F. v. M.	6
E. Woollsiana, F. v. M.	47
E. Youngii, F. v. M.	39
Myoporum Batae, F. v. M.	59
M. Beckeri, F. v. M.	57
M. brevipes, Bentham	63
M. Dampieri, Cunningham	69
M. debile, R. Brown	61
M. deserti, Cunningham	68
M. floribundum, Cunningham	58
M. glabrum, F. v. M.	70
M. humile, R. Brown	62
M. insulare, R. Brown	72
M. laxiflorum, Bentham	67
M. oppositifolium, R. Brown	64
M. platycarpum, R. Brown	60
M. salsoloides, Turczaninow	56
M. serratum, R. Brown	65
M. tenuifolium, Forster	71
M. viscosum, R. Brown	66

SYSTEMATIC AND GEOGRAPHIC INDEX.

#	Species	W.A.	S.A.			N.S.W.	Q.	N.A.
1	Eremophila Macdonnellii, F. v. M. Rep. Babb. Exped. 18 (1858)	W.A.	S.A.	—	—	N.S.W.	Q.	N.A.
2	E. Goodwinii, F. v. M. Rep. Babb. Exped. 17 (1857)	—	S.A.	—	—	N.S.W.	Q.	N.A.
3	E. Hughesii, F. v. M. fragm. viii. 228 (1874)	W.A.	S.A.	—	—	—	—	—
4	E. Giltesii, F. v. M. fragm. viii. 49 (1873)	—	S.A.	—	—	—	—	—
5	E. Drummondii, F. v. M. fragm. vi. 147 (1868)	W.A.	—	—	—	—	—	—
6	E. Willsii, F. v. M. fragm. iii. 21, t. 20 (1862)	W.A.	S.A.	—	—	—	—	—
7	E. Elderi, F. v. M. fragm. viii. 228 (1874)	W.A.	S.A.	—	—	—	—	—
8	E. Fraseri, F. v. M. fragm. xi. 51 (1878)	W.A.	—	—	—	—	—	N.A.
9	E. rotundifolia, F. v. M. fragm. i. 207 (1859)	—	S.A.	—	—	—	—	—
10	E. platycalyx, F. v. M. fragm. v. 109 (1866)	W.A.	S.A.	—	—	—	—	—
11	E. Freelingii, F. v. M. in Proceed. Roy. Soc. Tasm. iii. 295 (1858)	W.A.	S.A.	—	—	N.S.W.	—	—
12	E. graciliflora, F. v. M. fragm. i. 208 (1858)	W.A.	—	—	—	—	—	—
13	E. longifolia, F. v. M. in Proceed. Roy. Soc. Tasm. iii. 295 (1858)	W.A.	S.A.	—	V.	N.S.W.	Q.	N.A.
14	E. Laanii, F. v. M. in Melb. Chemist (Jan. 1885)	W.A.	—	—	—	—	—	—
15	E. bignoniflora, F. v. M. in Proceed. Roy. Soc. Tasm. iii. 294 (1858)	—	S.A.	—	V.	N.S.W.	Q.	N.A.
16	E. polyclada, F. v. M. in Proceed. Roy. Soc. Tasm. iii. 294 (1858)	—	S.A.	—	V.	N.S.W.	Q.	—
17	E. erinocalyx, F. v. M. fragm. i. 236 (1859)	W.A.	—	—	—	—	—	—
18	E. Bowmani, F. v. M. fragm. ii. 139 (1863)	—	S.A.	—	—	N.S.W.	Q.	—
19	E. Maitlandi, F. v. M. in Benth. fl. Austr. v. 19 (1870)	W.A.	—	—	—	—	—	—
20	E. Forrestii, F. v. M. fragm. vii. 49 (1869)	W.A.	—	—	—	—	—	—
21	E. leucophylla, Bentham fl. Austr. v. 18 (1870)	W.A.	—	—	—	—	—	—
22	E. Mackinlayi, F. v. M. fragm. iv. 80 (1864)	—	—	—	—	—	—	—
23	E. strongylophylla, F. v. M. fragm. x. 87 (1876)	—	—	—	—	N.S.W.	Q.	—
24	E. oppositifolia, R. Brown prodr. 518 (1810)	W.A.	S.A.	—	V.	N.S.W.	—	—
25	E. Mitchelli, Bentham in Mitch. Trop. Austr. 31 (1848)	—	S.A.	—	—	N.S.W.	Q.	—
26	E. Paisleyi, F. v. M. Rep. Babb. Exped. 17 (1858)	—	S.A.	—	—	—	—	—
27	E. Sturtii, R. Brown Appendix to Sturt's Exped. 22 (1849)	—	S.A.	—	—	N.S.W.	Q.	—
28	E. exilifolia, F. v. M. fragm. x. 88 (1876)	W.A.	S.A.	—	—	—	—	—
29	E. Gibsoni, F. v. M. fragm. viii. 227 (1874)	—	S.A.	—	—	—	—	—
30	E. Clarkei, F. v. M. fragm. i. 208 (1859)	W.A.	—	—	—	—	—	—
31	E. Latrobei, F. v. M. in Proceed. Roy. Soc. Tasm. iii. 294 (1858)	W.A.	S.A.	—	—	N.S.W.	Q.	N.A.
32	E. alternifolia, R. Brown prodr. 518 (1810)	W.A.	S.A.	—	V.	N.S.W.	—	—
33	E. latifolia, F. v. M. in Schlechtend. Linnæa xxv. 428 (1852)	W.A.	—	—	—	N.S.W.	—	—
34	E. denticulata, F. v. M. fragm. i. 125 (1859)	W.A.	S.A.	—	—	—	—	—
35	E. maculata, F. v. M. in Proceed. Roy. Soc. Tasm. iii. 297 (1858)	W.A.	S.A.	—	V.	N.S.W.	Q.	N.A.
36	E. Duttoni, F. v. M. Rep. Babb. Exped. 16 (1858)	—	S.A.	—	—	N.S.W.	Q.	—
37	E. Oldfieldi, F. v. M. fragm. i. 208 (1859)	W.A.	—	—	—	—	—	—
38	E. Brownii, F. v. M. in Proceed. Roy. Soc. Tasm. iii. 297 (1858)	W.A.	S.A.	—	V.	N.S.W.	Q.	N.A.
39	E. Youngii, F. v. M. fragm. x. 16 (1876)	W.A.	—	—	—	—	—	—
40	E. scoparia, F. v. M. in Proceed. Roy. Soc. Tasm. iii. 296 (1858)	—	S.A.	—	V.	N.S.W.	—	—
41	E. Dalyana, F. v. M. fragm. v. 22 (1865)	—	S.A.	—	—	N.S.W.	—	—
42	E. Pantoni, F. v. M. in Wing's South. Sc. Record ii. 251 (1882)	—	—	—	—	—	—	N.A.
43	E. Delisseri, F. v. M. fragm. v. 108, t. 42 (1865)	W.A.	S.A.	—	—	—	—	—
44	E. Behriana, F. v. M. in Proceed. Roy. Soc. Tasm. iii. 296 (1858)	—	S.A.	—	—	—	—	—
45	E. brevifolia, F. v. M. fragm. i. 126 (1859)	W.A.	—	—	—	—	—	—
46	E. crassifolia, F. v. M. in Proceed. Roy. Soc. Tasm. iii. 297 (1858)	—	S.A.	—	—	—	—	—
47	E. Woollsiana, F. v. M. fragm. i. 125, t. 7 (1859)	W.A.	—	—	—	—	—	—
48	E. microtheca, F. v. M. in Benth. fl. Austr. v. 14 (1870)	W.A.	—	—	—	—	—	—

SYSTEMATIC AND GEOGRAPHIC INDEX.

49 Eremophila densifolia, F. v. M. fragm. ii. 160 (1861)	W.A.	—	—	—	—	—	—
50 E. Weldii, F. v. M. fragm. vii. 109 (1870)	W.A.	S.A.	—	—	—	—	—
51 E. Dempsteri, F. v. M. fragm. x. 60 (1876)	W.A.	S.A.	—	—	—	—	—
52 E. gibbosifolia, F. v. M. Rep. Babb. Exped. 18 (1858)	—	S.A.	—	V.	—	—	—
53 E. adenotricha, F. v. M. in Benth. fl. Austr. v. 14 (1870)	W.A.	—	—	—	—	—	—
54 E. santalina, F. v. M. in Proceed. Roy. Soc. Tasm. iii. 295 (1858)	—	S.A.	—	—	—	—	—
55 E. divaricata, F. v. M. in Proceed. Roy. Soc. Tasm. iii. 293 (1858)	—	S.A.	—	V.	N.S.W.	Q.	—
56 Myoporum salsoloides, Turczaninow in Bull. de Mosc. xxxvi. 226 (1863)	W.A.	—	—	—	—	—	—
57 M. Beckeri, F. v. M. in Benth. fl. Austr. v. 7 (1870)	W.A.	—	—	—	—	—	—
58 M. floribundum, Cunningham in Hueg. enum. 78 (1837)	—	—	—	V.	N.S.W.	—	—
59 M. Batae, F. v. M. in Proceed. Linn. Soc. N.S.W. vi. 792 (1881)	—	—	—	—	N.S.W.	—	—
60 M. platycarpum, R. Brown prodr. 516 (1810)	W.A.	S.A.	—	V.	N.S.W.	Q.	—
61 M. debile, R. Brown prodr. 516 (1810)	—	—	—	—	N.S.W.	Q.	—
62 M. humile, R. Brown prodr. 516 (1810)	W.A.	S.A.	T.	V.	N.S.W.	—	—
63 M. brevipes, Bentham fl. Austr. v. 6 (1870)	—	S.A.	—	—	—	—	—
64 M. oppositifolium, R. Brown prodr. 516 (1810)	W.A.	—	—	—	—	—	—
65 M. serratum, R. Brown prodr. 516 (1810)	W.A.	—	—	—	—	—	—
66 M. viscosum, R. Brown prodr. 516 (1810)	—	S.A.	—	V.	N.S.W.	—	—
67 M. laxiflorum, Bentham Flora Austr. v. 6 (1870)	—	—	—	—	—	Q.	—
68 M. deserti, Cunningham in Hueg. enum. 78 (1837)	W.A.	S.A.	—	V.	N.S.W.	Q.	—
69 M. Dampieri, Cunningham in Cand. prodr. xi. 708 (1847)	W.A.	S.A.	—	V.	N.S.W.	Q.	N.A.
70 M. glabrum, F. v. M. third suppl. Cens. Austr. pl. (1886)	—	—	—	—	N.S.W.	Q.	—
71 M. tenuifolium, Forster fl. ins. Austr. prodr. 44 (1786)	—	—	—	—	N.S.W.	Q.	—
72 M. insulare, R. Brown prodr. 515 (1810)	W.A.	S.A.	T.	V.	N.S.W.	—	—
Supplement.							
1 Eremophila viscida, Endlicher nov. stirp. dec. 51 (1839)	W.A.	—	—	—	—	—	—
2 E. resinosa, F. v. M. in Proceed. Roy. Soc. Tasm. iii. 296 (1858)	W.A.	—	—	—	—	—	—

PLATES.

Eremophila Macdonnelli.

F. v. M. in Report on plants of Babbage's Expedition 18 (1858).

PLATE I.

Figure 1, branched hairs of the general vestiture.
    2, flower-bud.
    3, unexpanded flower.
    4, expanded flower.
    5, corolla laid open.
    6, stamens, front- and back-view.
    7, pollen-grains.
    8, calyx with pistil.
    9, style and ovary.
    10, fruit-bearing calyx.
    11, side-view of fruit.
    12, transverse section of fruit.
    13, longitudinal section of fruit.
    14, seeds.
    15, embryo.

All magnified, except fig. 8, but to very various extent.

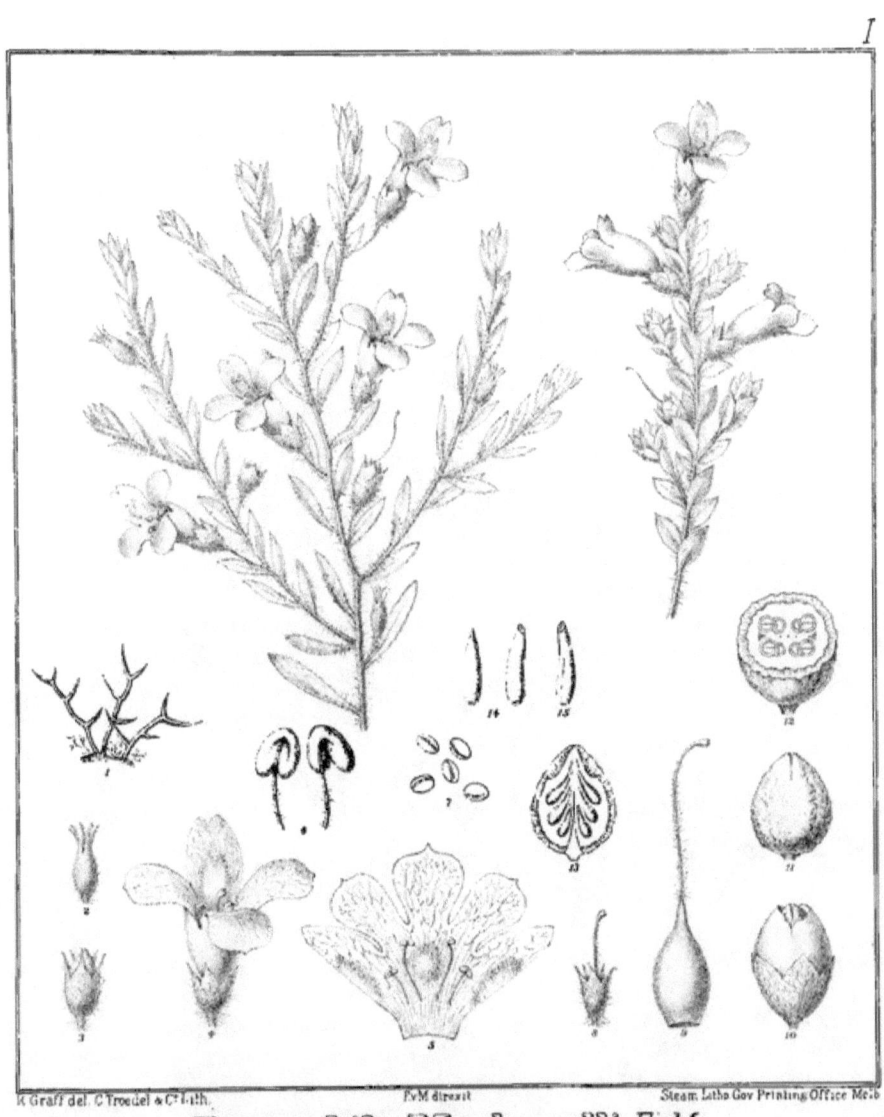
Eremophila Macdonnelli F.v.M.

Eremophila Goodwini.

F. v. M. in Report on plants of Babbage's Expedition 17 (1858).

PLATE II.

Figure 1, gland-bearing hairs of the general vestiture.

    2, unexpanded flower.

    3, expanded flower.

    4, corolla laid open.

    5, stamens, front- and back-view.

    6, calyx with pistil.

    7, side-view of fruit.

    8, fruit, the pericarp removed.

    9, transverse section of fruit.

    10, longitudinal section of fruit.

    11, seeds.

        All more or less enlarged.

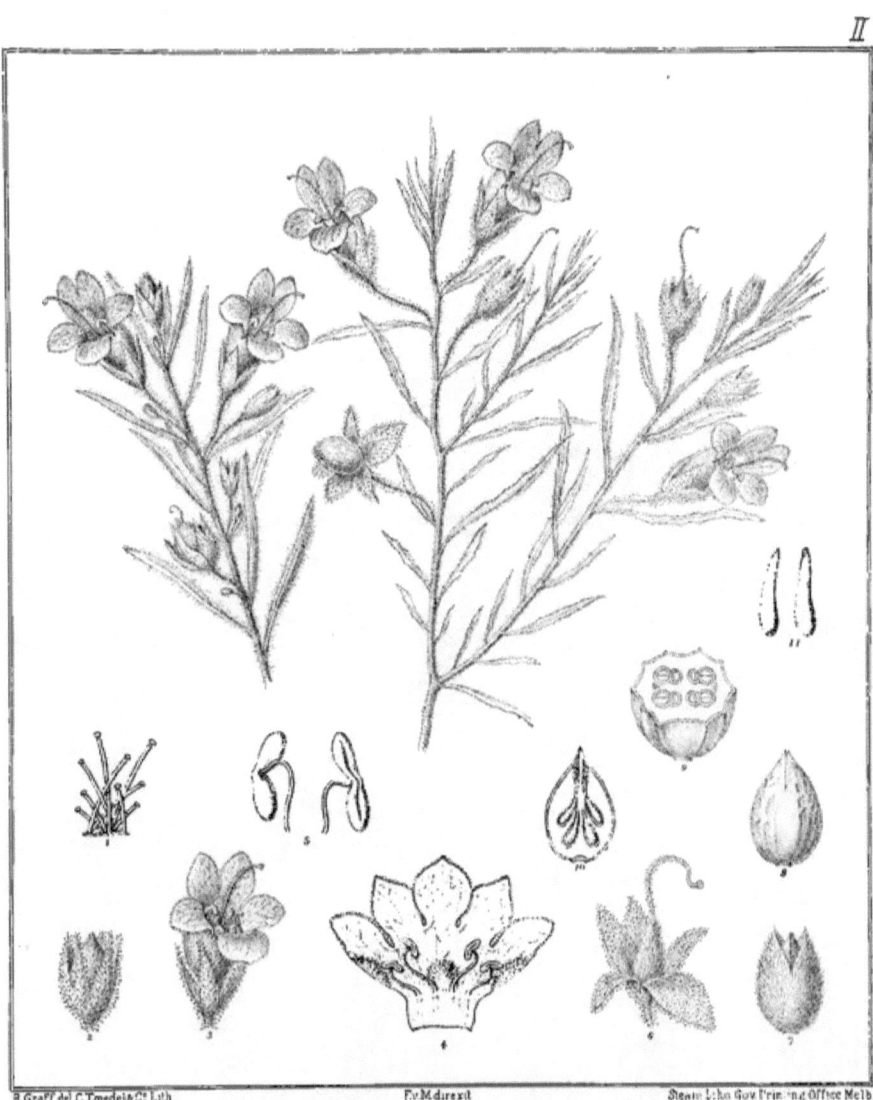

Eremophila Goodwinii F.v.M.

Eremophila Hughesii.

F. v. M. Fragmenta phytographiæ Australiæ viii. 228 (1874).

PLATE III.

Figure 1, unexpanded flower.

    2, expanded flower.

    3, corolla laid open.

    4, anthers with portion of filament, front- and back-view.

    5, calyx with pistil.

    6, side-view of fruit.

    7, fruit, the pericarp removed.

    8, transverse section of fruit.

    9, longitudinal section of fruit.

10, seeds.

    All magnified, but to different degree.

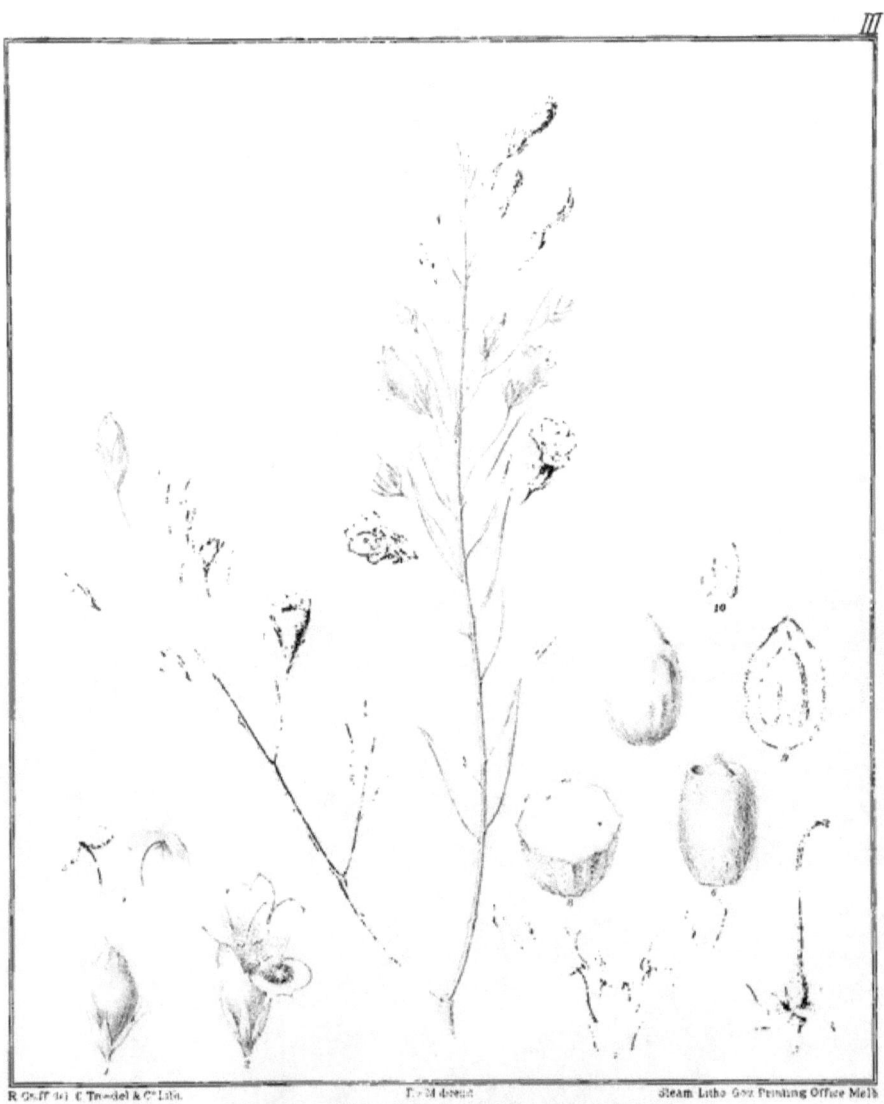

Eremophila Hughesii FvM

Eremophila Gilesii.

F. v. M. Fragmenta phytographiæ Australiæ viii. 49 (1873).

PLATE IV.

Figure 1, unexpanded flower.

2, expanded flower.

3, corolla laid open.

4, stamens, front- and back-view.

5, calyx with pistil.

6, side-view of fruit.

7, transverse section of fruit.

8, longitudinal section of fruit.

All enlarged, but to various extent.

Eremophila Gilesii FvM

Eremophila Drummondii.

F. v. M. Fragmenta phytographiæ Australiæ vi. 147 (1868).

PLATE V.

Figure 1, unexpanded flower.

2, expanded flower.

3, corolla laid open.

4, stamens, front- and back-view.

5, calyx with pistil.

6, side-view of fruit.

7, fruit seen from beneath.

8, transverse section of fruit.

9, longitudinal section of fruit.

All enlarged, but in various degree.

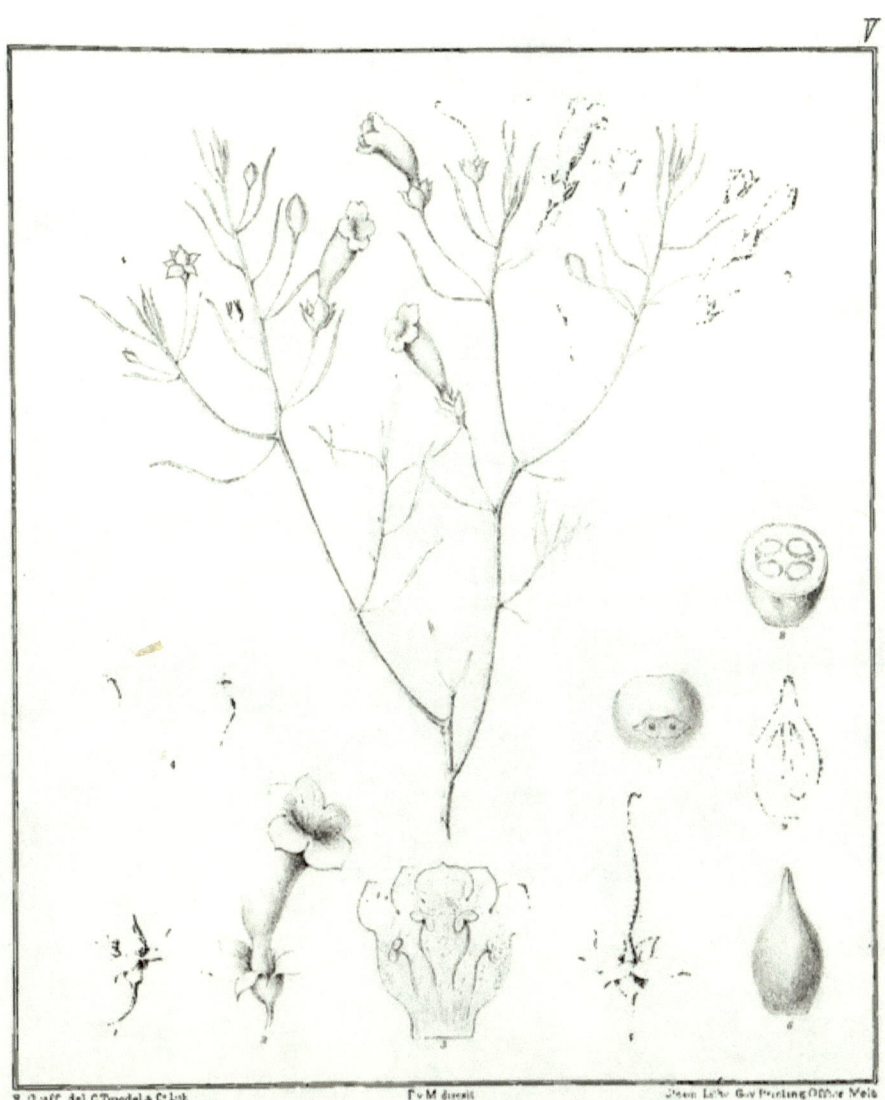

Eremophila Drummondii F.v.M

Eremophila Willsii.

F. v. M. Fragmenta phytographiæ Australiæ iii. 21, t. 20 (1862).

PLATE VI.

Figure 1, hairs of vestiture.

2, unexpanded flower.

3, expanded flower.

4, corolla laid open.

5, stamens, front- and back-view.

6, calyx with pistil.

7, side-view of fruit.

8, transverse section of fruit.

9, longitudinal section of fruit.

10, seeds.

All enlarged, but in various degree.

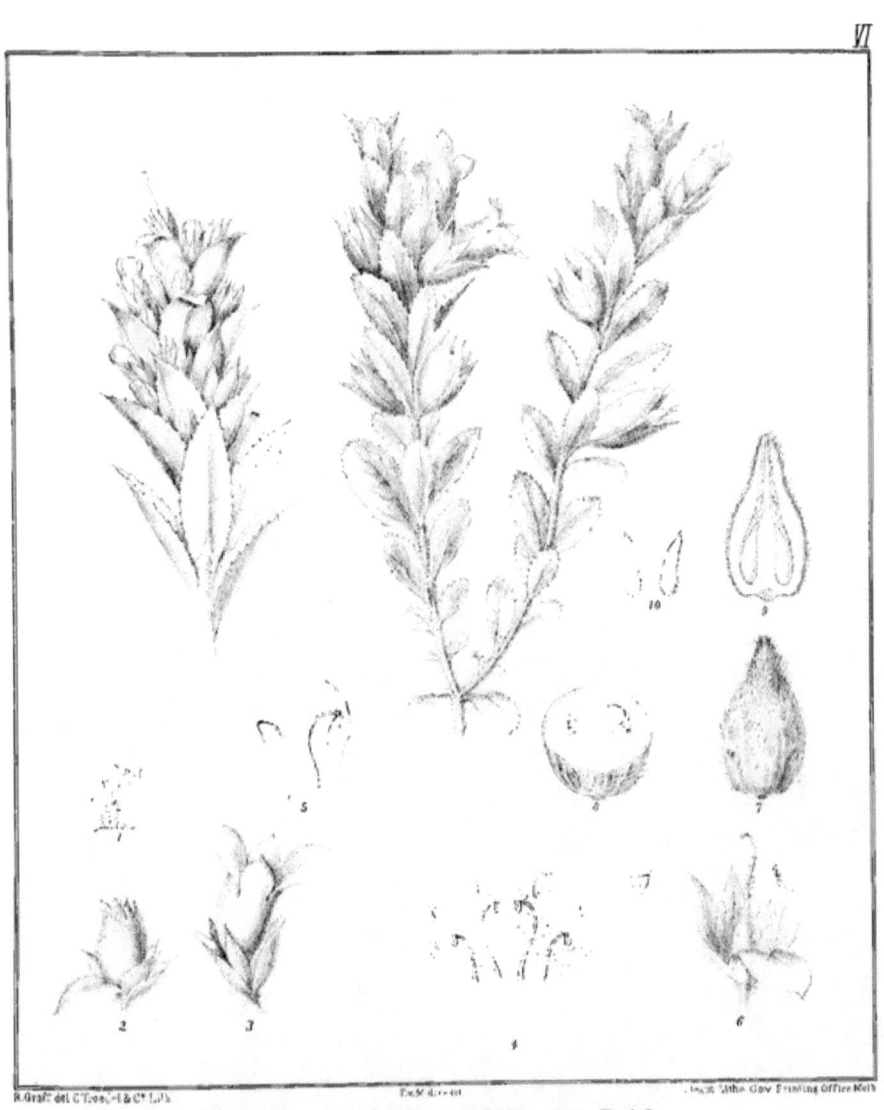

Eremophila Willsii F.v.M.

Eremophila Elderi.

F. v. M. Fragmenta phytographiæ Australiæ viii. 228 (1874).

PLATE VII.

Figure 1, hairs of vestiture.

    2, flower-bud.

    3, expanded flower.

    4, corolla laid open.

    5, stamens, front- and back-view.

    6, calyx with pistil.

    7, side-view of fruit.

    8, fruit, the pericarp removed.

    9, transverse section of fruit.

    10, longitudinal section of fruit.

    11, seeds.

All enlarged, but in various degree.

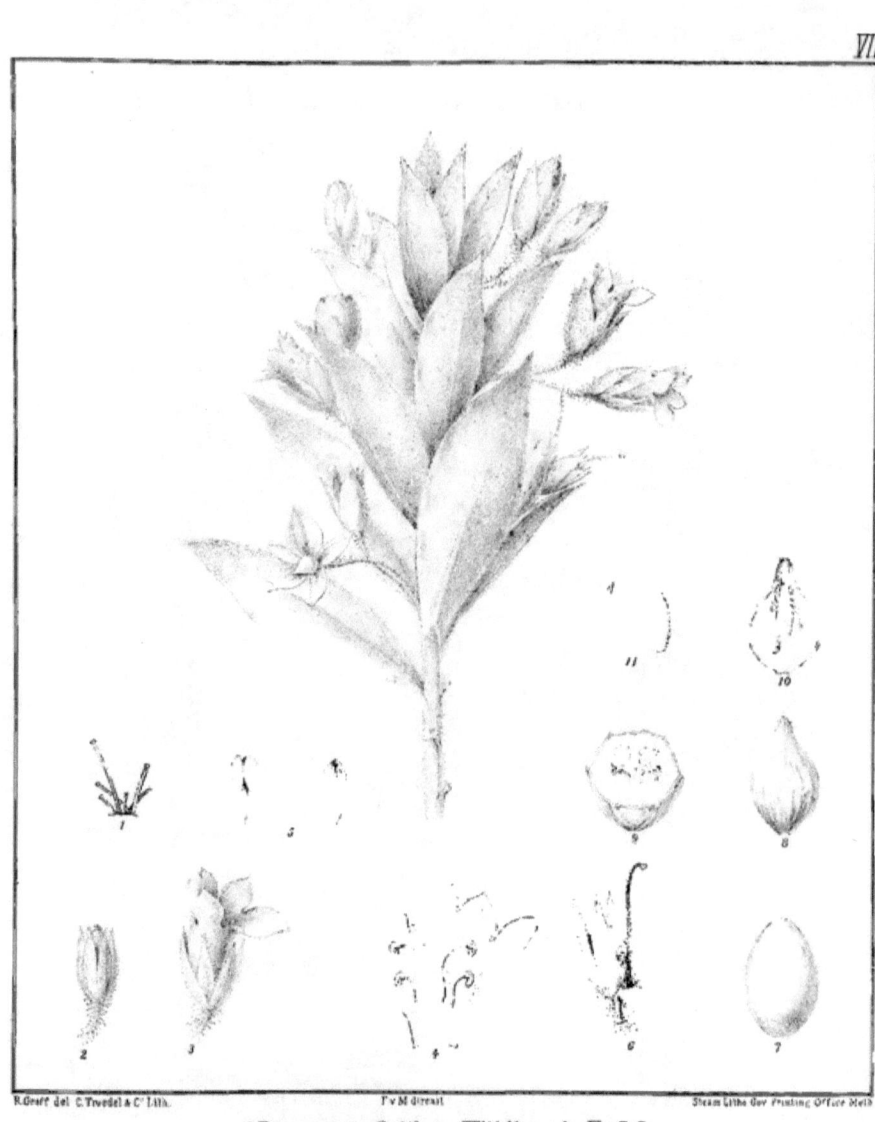

Eremophila Elderi F.v.M.

Eremophila Fraseri.

F. v. M. Fragmenta phytographiæ Australiæ xi. 51 (1878)

PLATE VIII.

Figure 1 and 2, flower-buds.

    3, expanded flower.

    4, corolla laid open.

    5, stamens, front- and back-view.

    6, calyx with pistil.

    7, fruit, side-view.

    8, fruit, seen from beneath.

    9, transverse section of fruit.

    10, longitudinal section of fruit.

    11, seeds.

All enlarged, but in various degree.

Eremophila Fraseri *F.v.M*

Eremophila rotundifolia.

F v. M. Fragmenta phytographiæ Australiæ i. 207 (1859).

PLATE IX.

Figure 1, flower-bud.

2, expanded flower.

3, corolla laid open.

4, stamens, front- and back-view.

5, calyx with pistil.

6, side-view of fruit.

7, fruit seen from beneath.

8, transverse section of fruit.

9, longitudinal section of fruit.

10, seeds.

All enlarged, but in various degree.

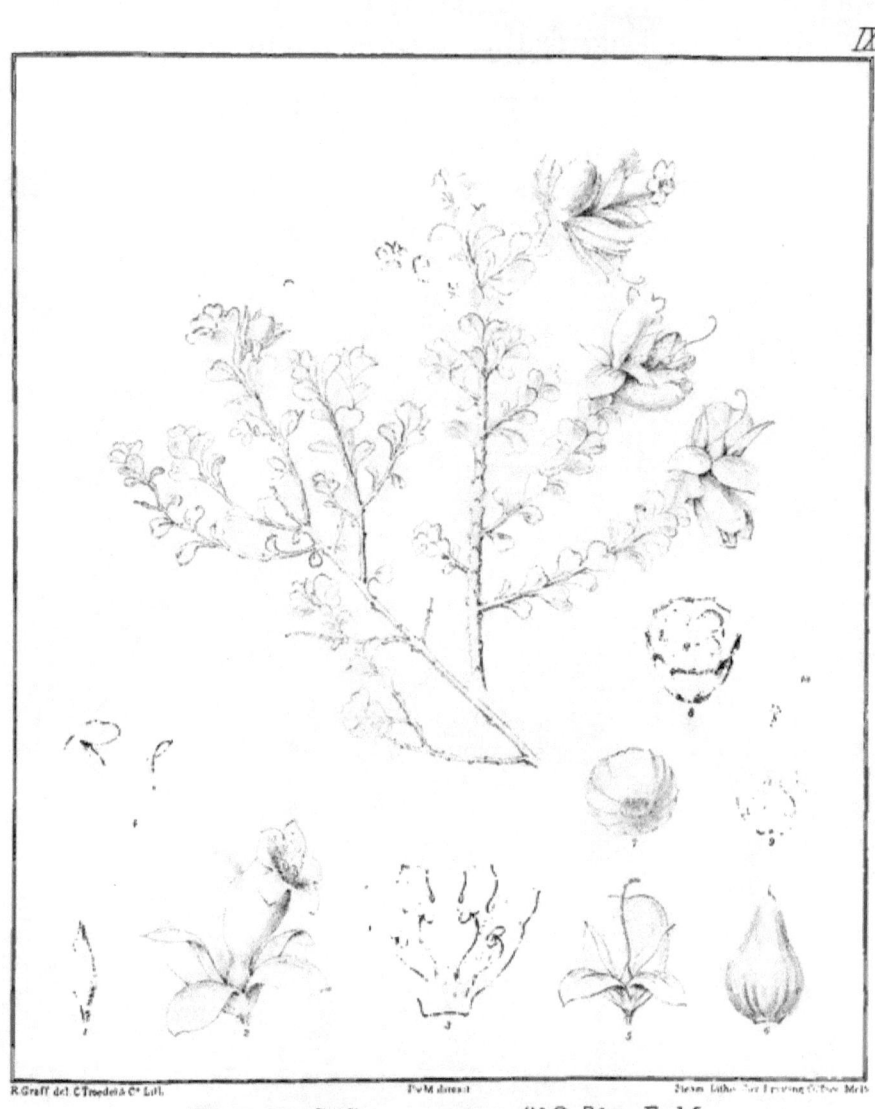

Eremophila rotundifolia *FvM*.

Eremophila platycalyx.

F. v. M. Fragmenta phytographiæ Australiæ v. 109 (1866).

PLATE X.

Figure 1, flower-bud.

    2, expanded flower.

    3, corolla laid open.

    4, stamens, front- and back-view.

    5, calyx with pistil.

    6, side-view of fruit.

    7, fruit seen from beneath.

    8, transverse section of fruit.

    9, longitudinal section of fruit.

    10, seeds.

All enlarged, but in various degree

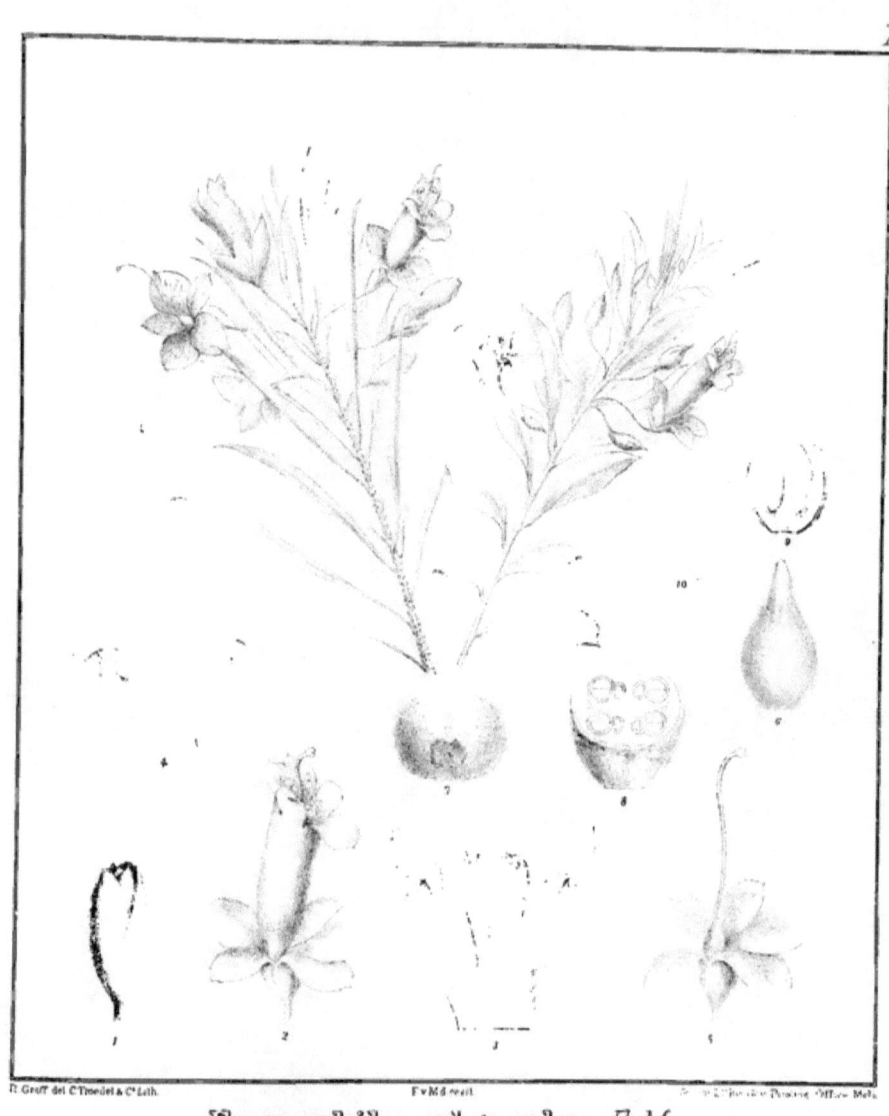

Eremophila platycalyx *FvM*

Eremophila Freelingii.

F. v. M. in Proceedings of the Royal Society of Tasmania iii. 295 (1858).

PLATE XI.

Figure 1, flower-bud.

2, unexpanded flower.

3, expanded flower.

4, corolla laid open.

5, stamens, front- and back-view.

6, calyx with pistil.

7, side-view of fruit.

8, fruit seen from beneath.

9, longitudinal section of fruit.

10, transverse section of fruit.

11, seeds.

All enlarged, but in various degree

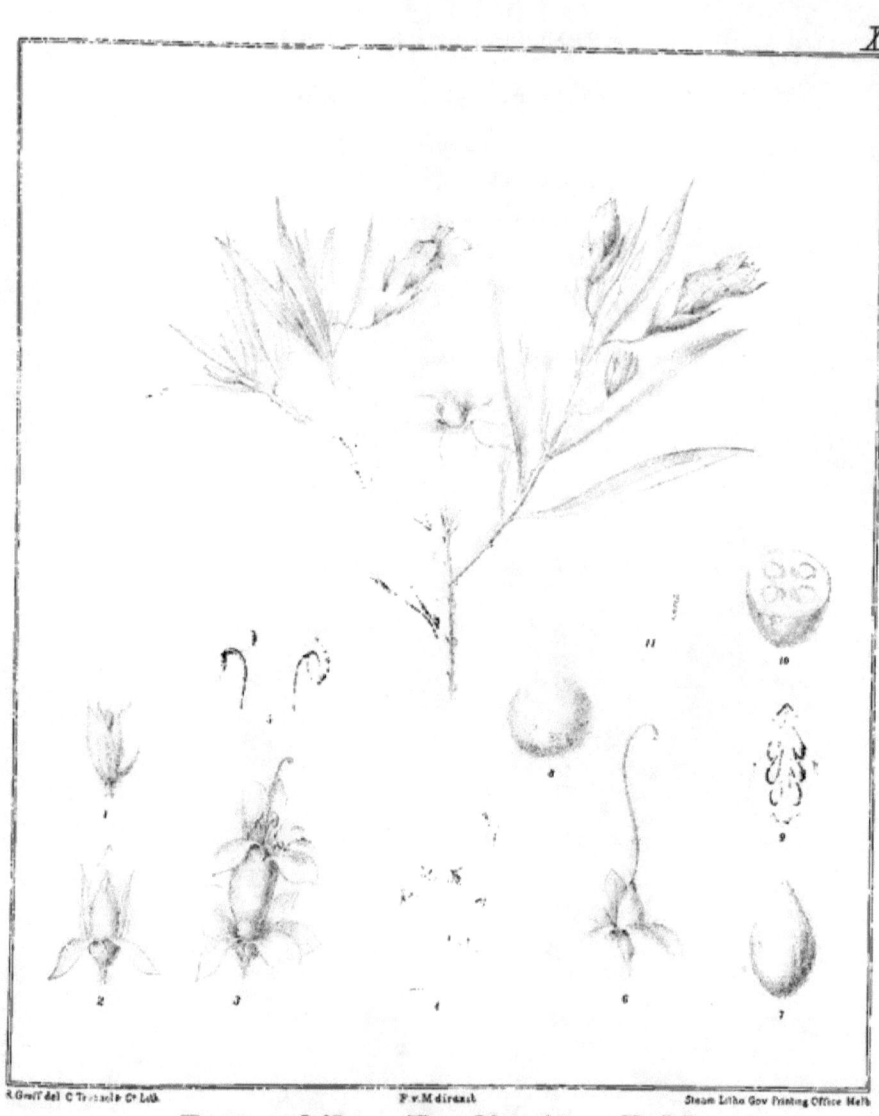

Eremophila Freelingii. *F.v.M.*

Eremophila graciliflora.

F. v. M. Fragmenta phytographiæ Australiæ i. 208 (1858).

PLATE XII.

Figure 1, a leaf.

2, flower-bud.

3, expanded flower.

4, corolla laid open.

5, stamens, front- and back-view.

6, pistil.

7, side-view of fruit.

8, the same, the pericarp removed.

9, fruit seen from beneath.

10, transverse section of fruit.

11, longitudinal section of fruit.

12, seeds.

All enlarged, but to a various degree.

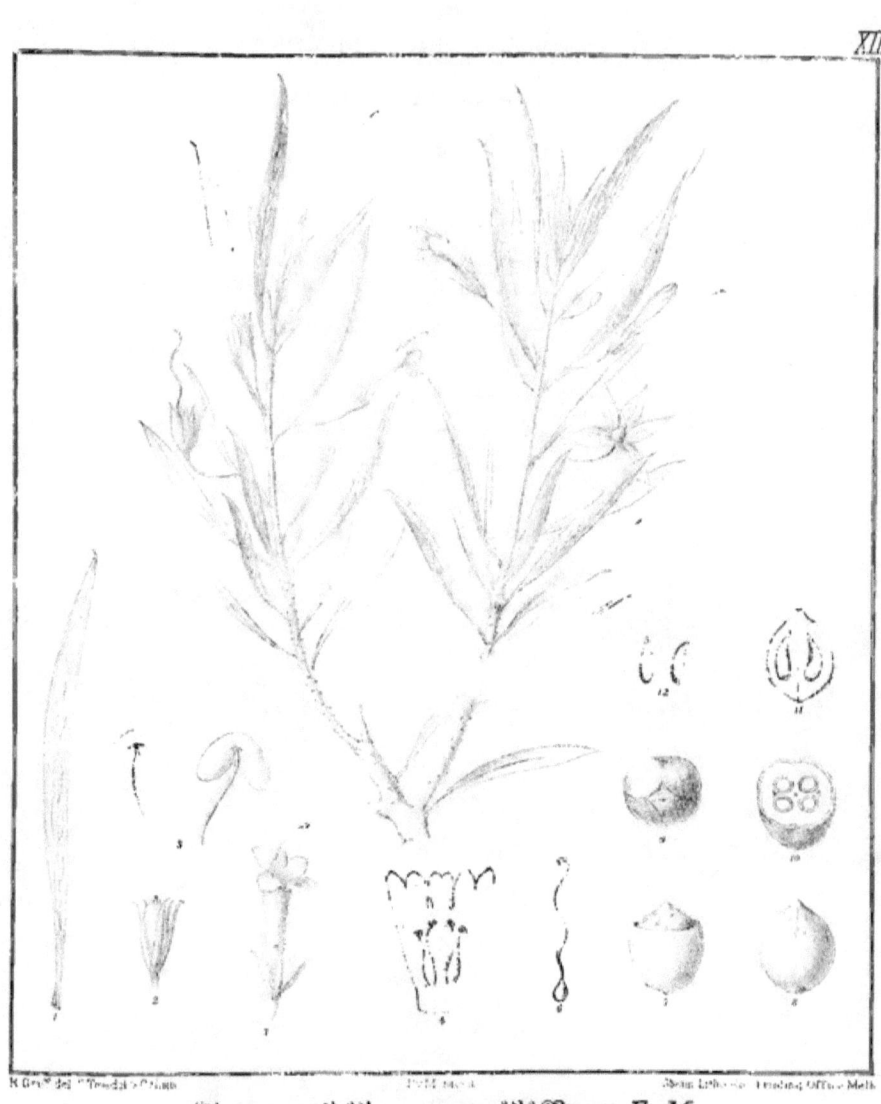

Eremophila graciliflora F.v.M.

EREMOPHILA LONGIFOLIA.

F. v. M. in Proceedings of the Royal Society of Tasmania iii. 295 (1858).

PLATE XIII.

Figure 1 and 2, unexpanded flowers.

      3, expanded flower.

      4, corolla laid open.

      5, stamens, front- and back-view.

      6, calyx with pistil.

      7, fruit with calyx, portion of the pericarp removed.

      8, fruit, the outer layer of the pericarp removed.

      9, transverse section of fruit.

      10, longitudinal section of fruit.

      11, seeds.

      12, embryo.

          All enlarged, but in various degree.

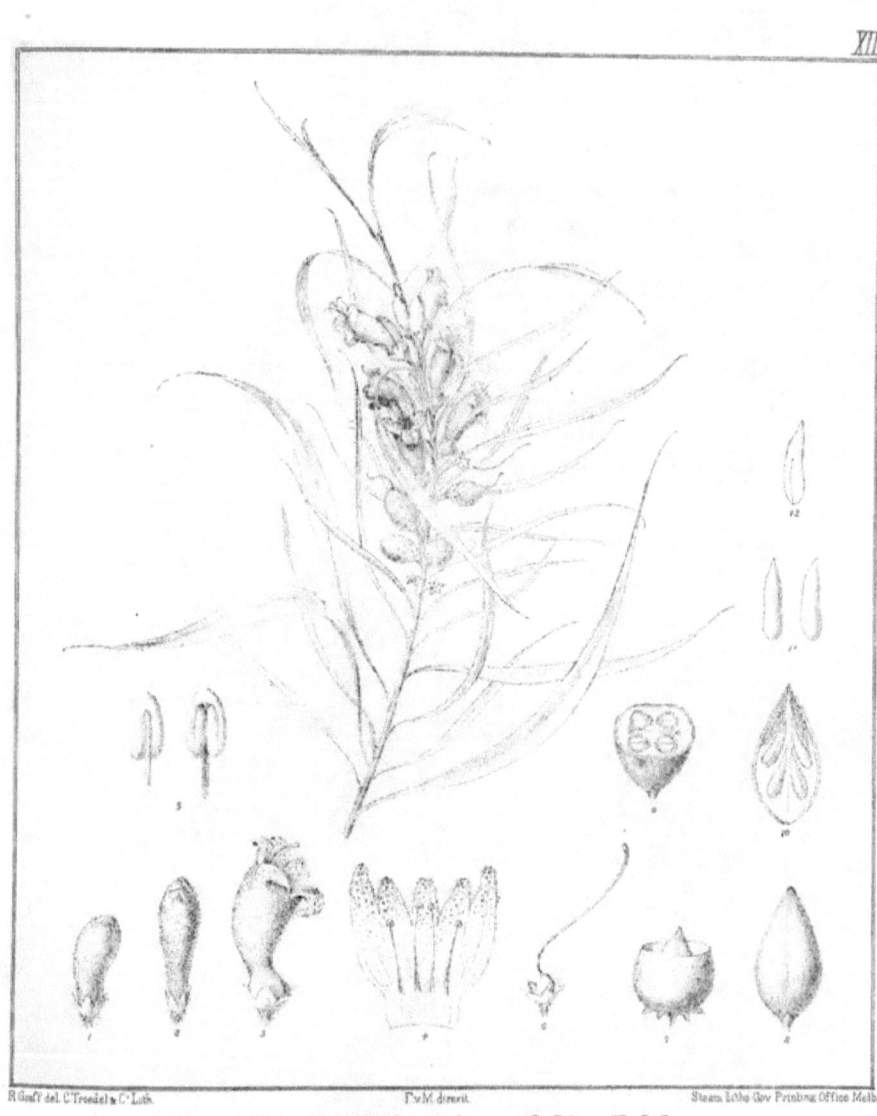

Eremophila longifolia FvM.

Eremophila Laanii.

F v. M. in Melbourne Chemist (Jan. 1885).

PLATE XIV.

Figure 1, unexpanded flower.

2, expanded flower.

3, corolla laid open.

4, stamens, front- and back-view.

5, pistil.

6, side-view of fruit.

7, transverse section of fruit.

8, longitudinal section of fruit.

All enlarged, but in various degree

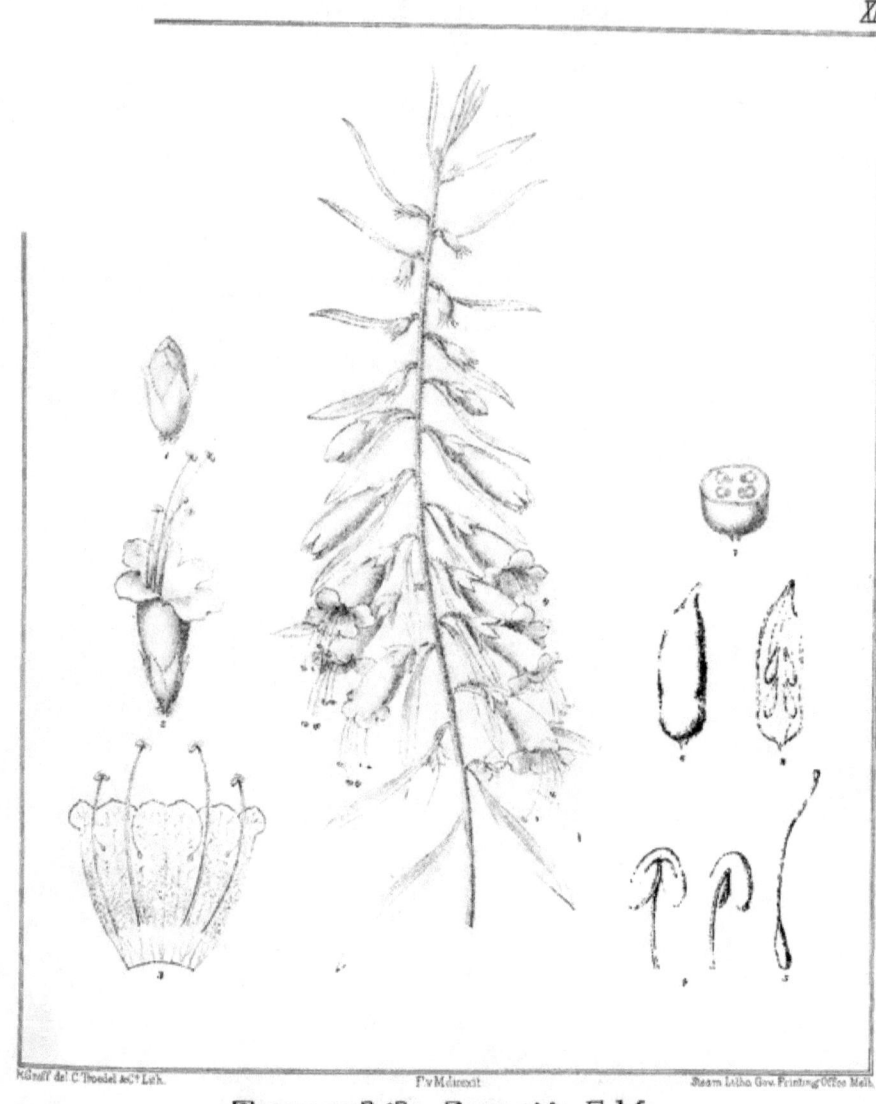

Eremophila Laanii F.vM

Eremophila bignoniflora.

F. v. M. in Proceedings of the Royal Society of Tasmania iii. 294 (1858).

PLATE XV.

Figure 1, flower-bud.
    2, unexpanded flower.
    3, expanded flower.
    4, corolla laid open.
    5, stamens, front- and back-view.
    6, calyx with pistil.
    7, side-view of fruit.
    8, lower half of fruit, seen from beneath.
    9, transverse section of fruit.
    10, longitudinal section of fruit.
    11, seeds.

Figures 5, 9, 10, 11, magnified, the rest of natural size.

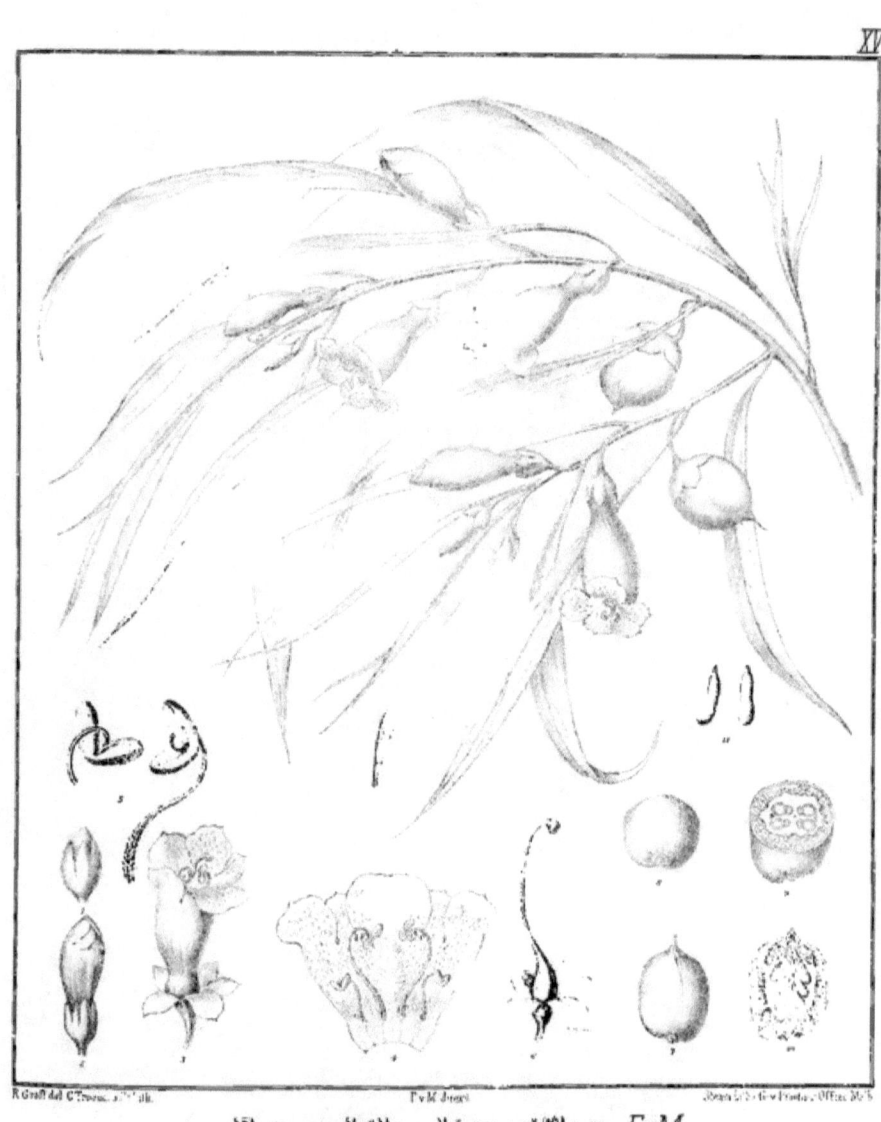

Eremophila bignoniflora FvM

Eremophila polyclada.

F. v. M. in Proceedings of the Royal Society of Tasmania iii. 294 (1858).

PLATE XVI.

Figure 1, flower-bud.

2, unexpanded flower.

3, expanded flower.

4, corolla laid open.

5, stamens, front- and back-view.

6, calyx with pistil.

7, side-view of fruit.

8, transverse section of fruit.

9, longitudinal section of fruit.

10, seeds.

All enlarged, but in various degree.

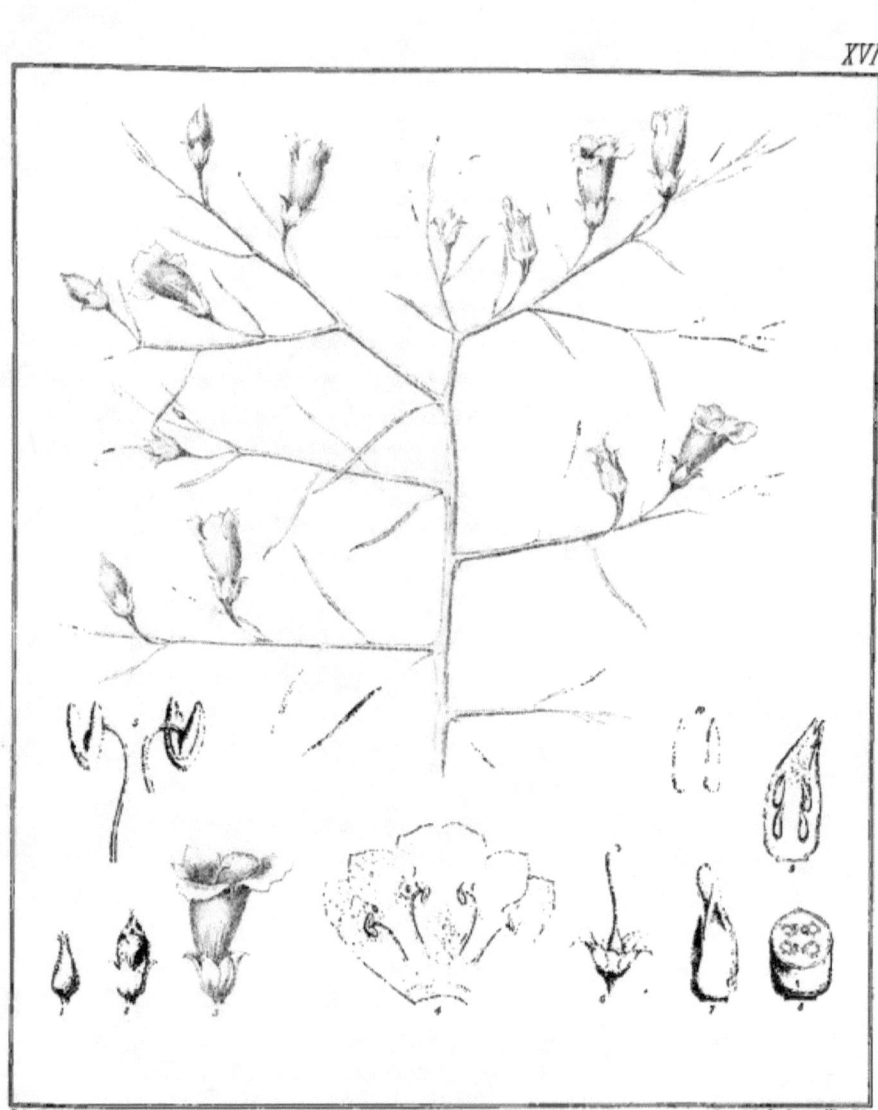

Eremophila polyclada F.vM.

Eremophila eriocalyx.

F. v. M. Fragmenta phytographiæ Australiæ i. 236 (1859).

PLATE XVII.

Figure 1, branched hairs on calyx and its stalklet.

2, flower-bud.

3, unexpanded flower.

4, expanded flower.

5, corolla laid open.

6, stamens, front- and back-view.

7, calyx with pistil.

8, side-view of fruit.

9, lower half of fruit, seen from beneath.

10, transverse section of fruit.

11, longitudinal section of fruit.

12, seeds.

All enlarged, but in various degree.

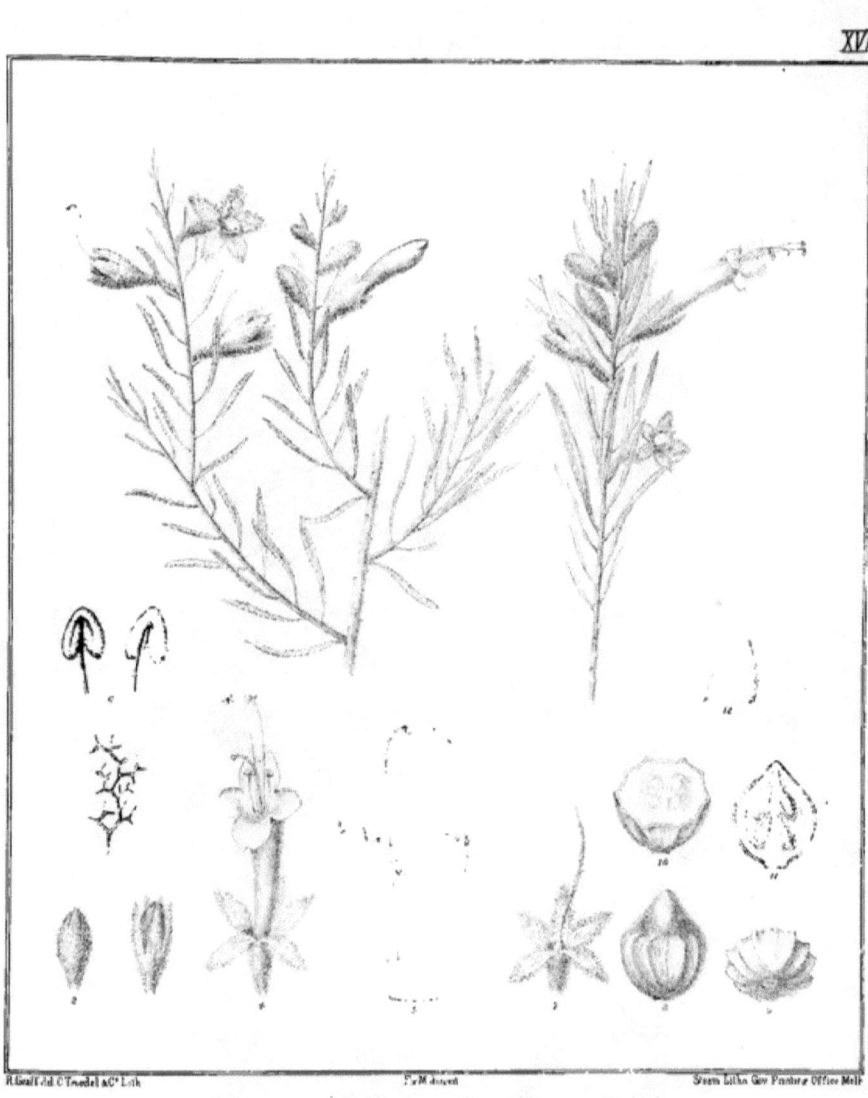

Eremophila eriocalyx F.v.M.

Eremophila Bowmanii.

F. v. M. Fragmenta phytographiæ Australiæ ii. 139 (1861).

PLATE XVIII.

Figure 1, flower-bud.

    2, expanded flower.

    3, corolla laid open.

    4, stamens, front- and back-view.

    5, pistil.

    6, side-view of fruit.

    7, lower half of fruit, seen from beneath.

    8, transverse section of fruit.

    9, longitudinal section of fruit.

    10, seeds.

All enlarged, but in various degree.

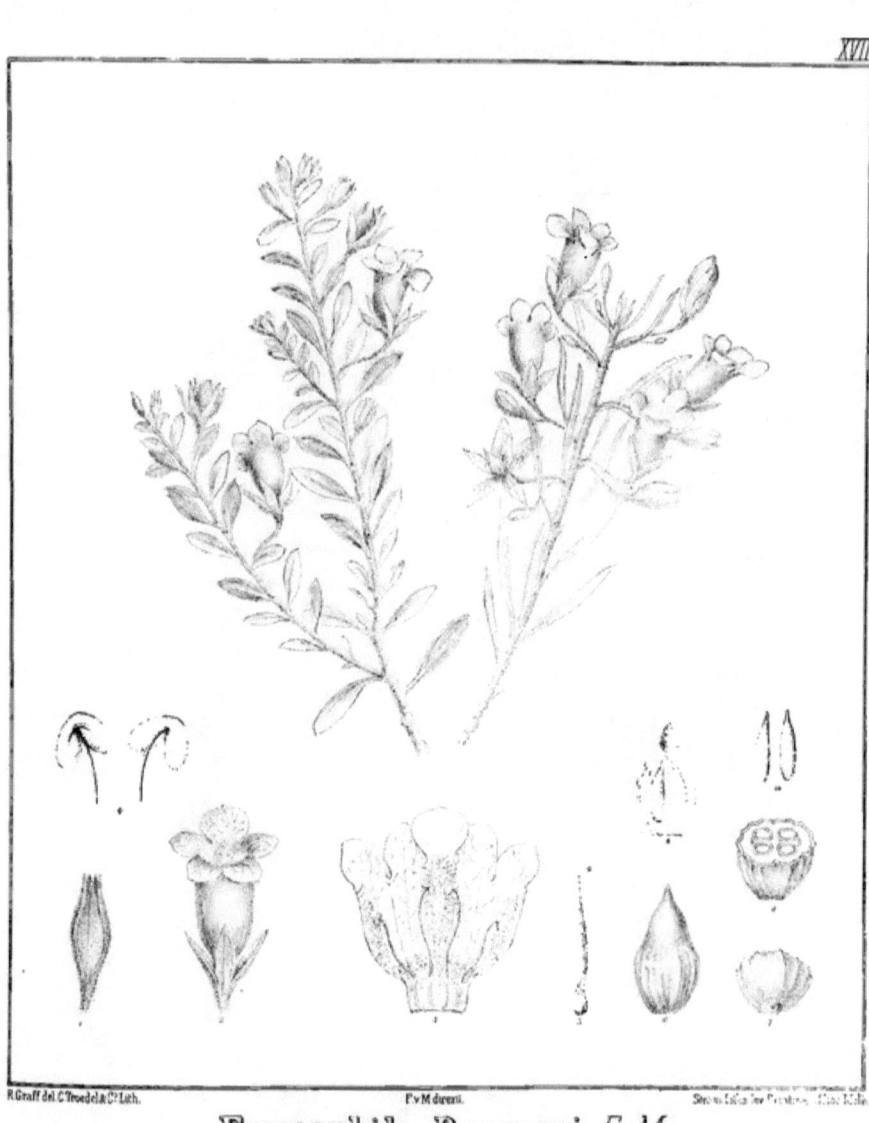

Eremophila Bowmani. F.vM.

Eremophila Maitlandi.

F. v. M. in Bentham's Flora Australiensis v. 19 (1870).

PLATE XIX.

Figure 1, a leaf.

2, hairs of vestiture.

3, flower-bud.

4, expanded flower.

5, corolla, laid open.

6, stamens, front- and back-view.

7, calyx with pistil.

8, side-view of fruit.

9, lower half of fruit, seen from beneath.

10, transverse section of fruit.

11, longitudinal section of fruit.

12, seeds.

All enlarged, but to a various degree.

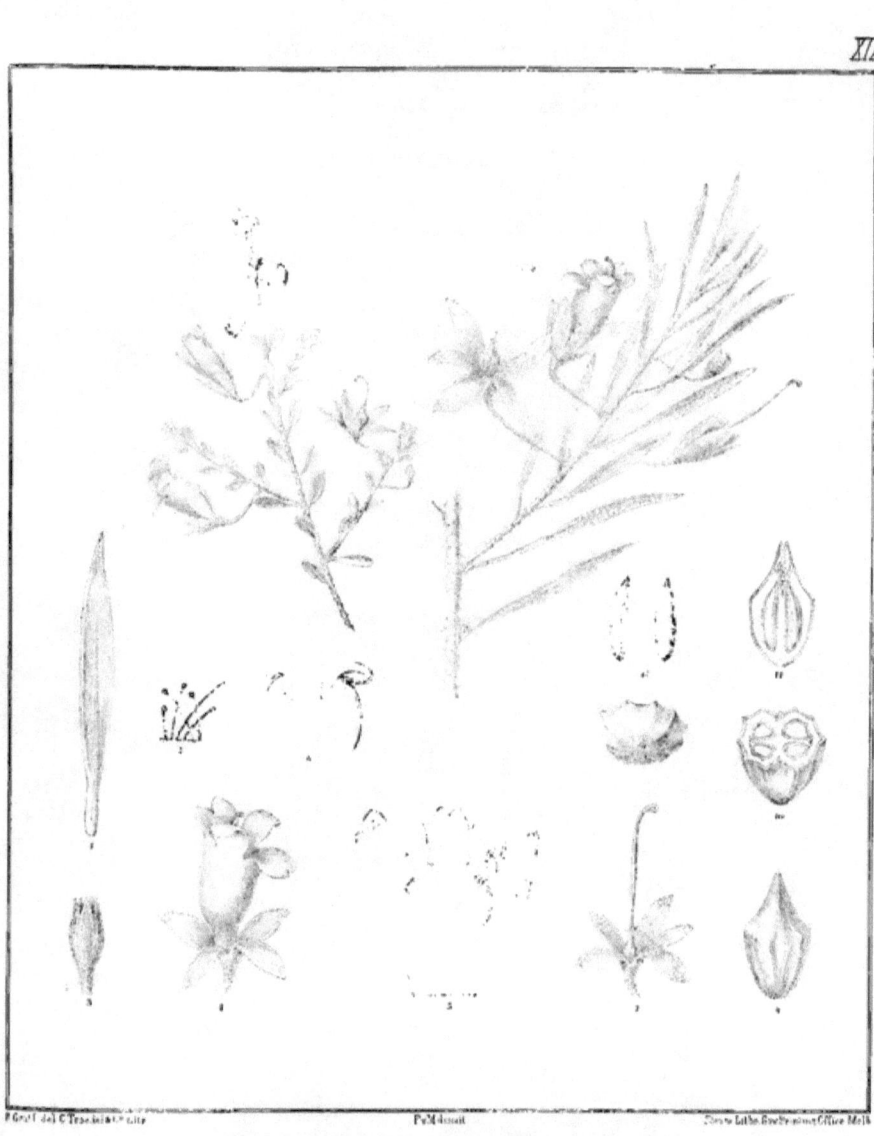

Eremophila Maitlandi. F.v.M.

Eremophila Forrestii.

F. v. M. Fragmenta phytographiæ Australiæ vii. 49 (1869).

PLATE XX.

Figure 1, branched hairs of vestiture.

2, unexpanded flower.

3, expanded flower.

4, corolla, laid open.

5, stamens, front- and back-view.

6, pistil.

7, side-view of fruit.

8, lower half of fruit, seen from beneath.

9, transverse section of fruit.

10, longitudinal section of fruit.

11, seeds.

All enlarged, but to a various degree.

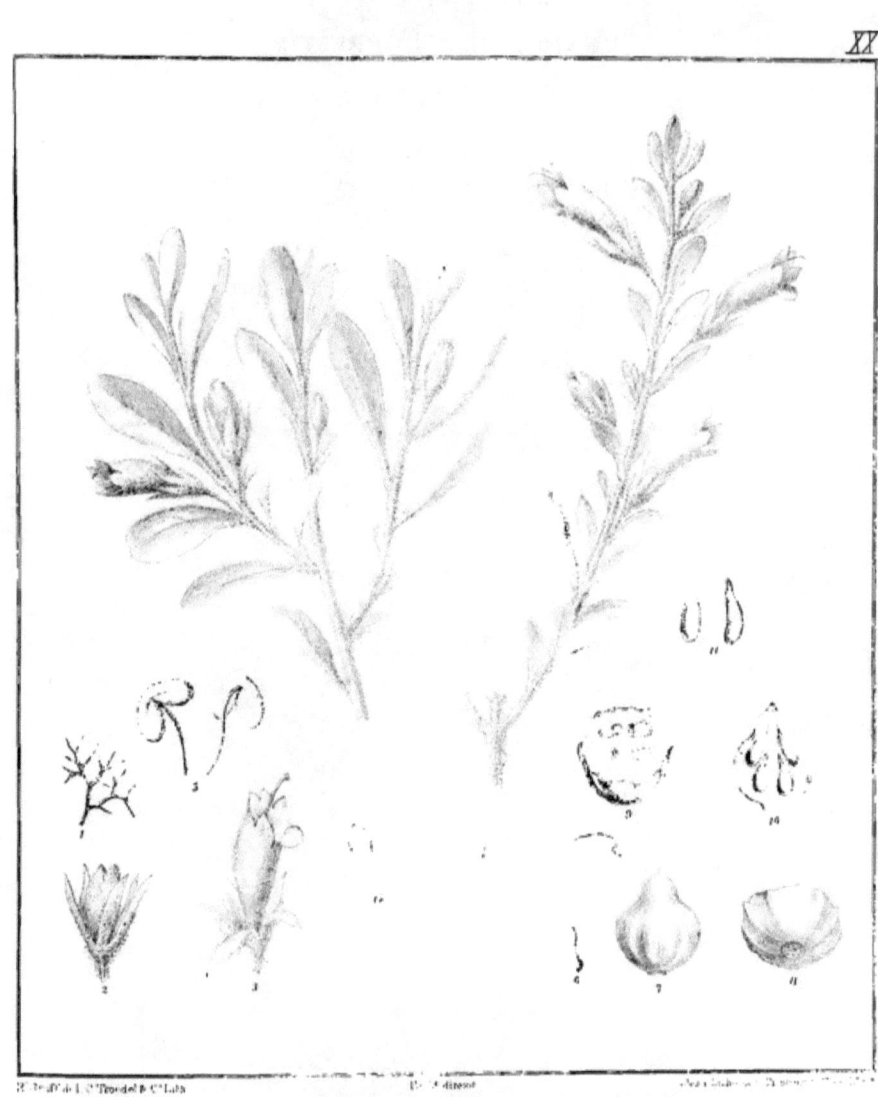

Eremophila Forrestii F.v.M.

Eremophila leucophylla.

Bentham, Flora Australiensis v. 18 (1870).

PLATE XXI.

Figure 1, branched hairs of vestiture.

2, flower-bud.

3, unexpanded flower.

4, expanded flower.

5, corolla, laid open.

6, stamens, front- and back-view.

7, pistil.

8, fruit, the outer layer of the pericarp partially removed.

9, fruit, the outer layer of the pericarp entirely removed.

10, lower portion of fruit, seen from beneath.

11, transverse section of fruit.

12, longitudinal section of fruit.

13, seeds.

All more or less enlarged.

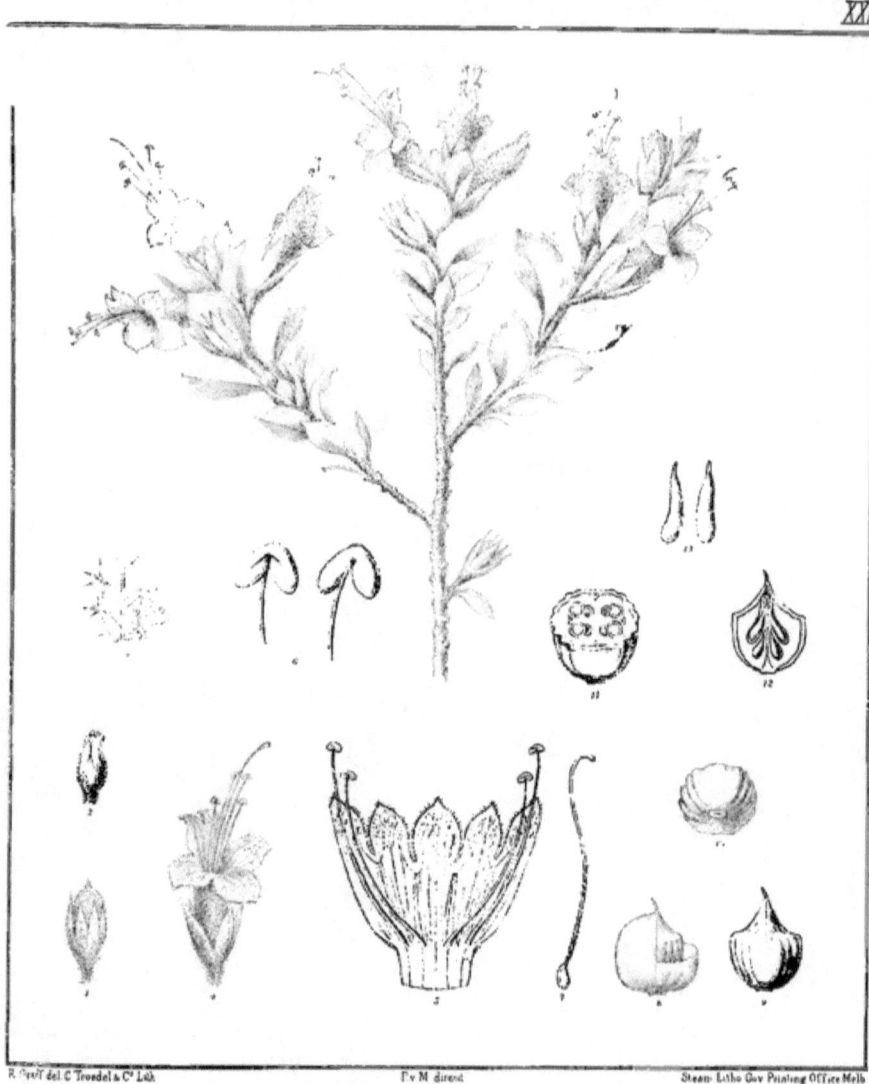

Eremophila leucophylla BENTHAM.

Eremophila Mackinlayi.

F. v. M. Fragmenta phytographiæ Australiæ iv. 80 (1864).

PLATE XXII.

Figure 1, unexpanded flower with a floral leaf.

2, expanded flower.

3, corolla, laid open.

4, stamens, front- and back-view.

5, pistil.

6, side-view of fruit.

7, lower part of fruit, seen from beneath.

8, transverse section of fruit.

9, longitudinal section of fruit.

All more or less enlarged.

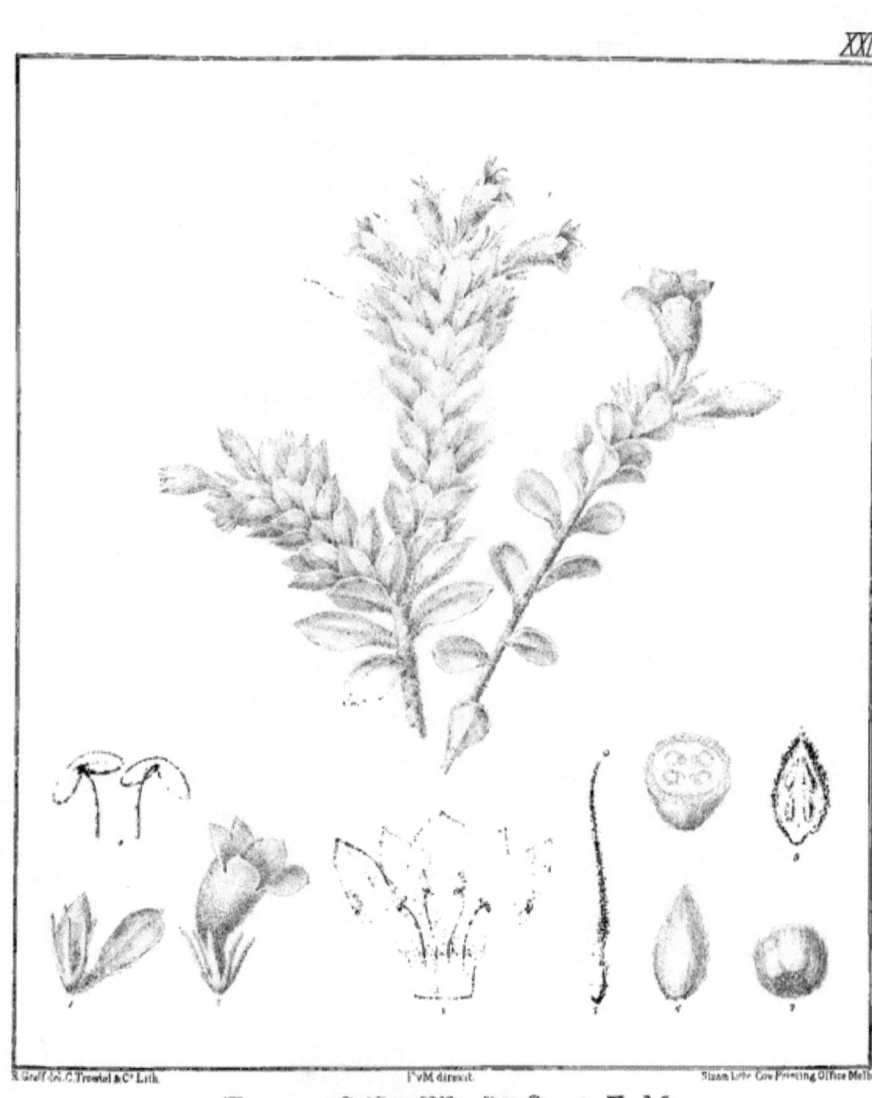

Eremophila Mackinlayi F.v.M.

Eremophila strongylophylla.

F. v. M. Fragmenta phytographiæ Australiæ x. 87 (1876).

PLATE XXIII.

Figure 1, flower-bud.

2, expanded flower.

3, corolla, laid open.

4, stamens, front- and back-view.

5, calyx with pistil.

6, side-view of young fruit.

7, young fruit, seen from beneath.

All more or less enlarged.

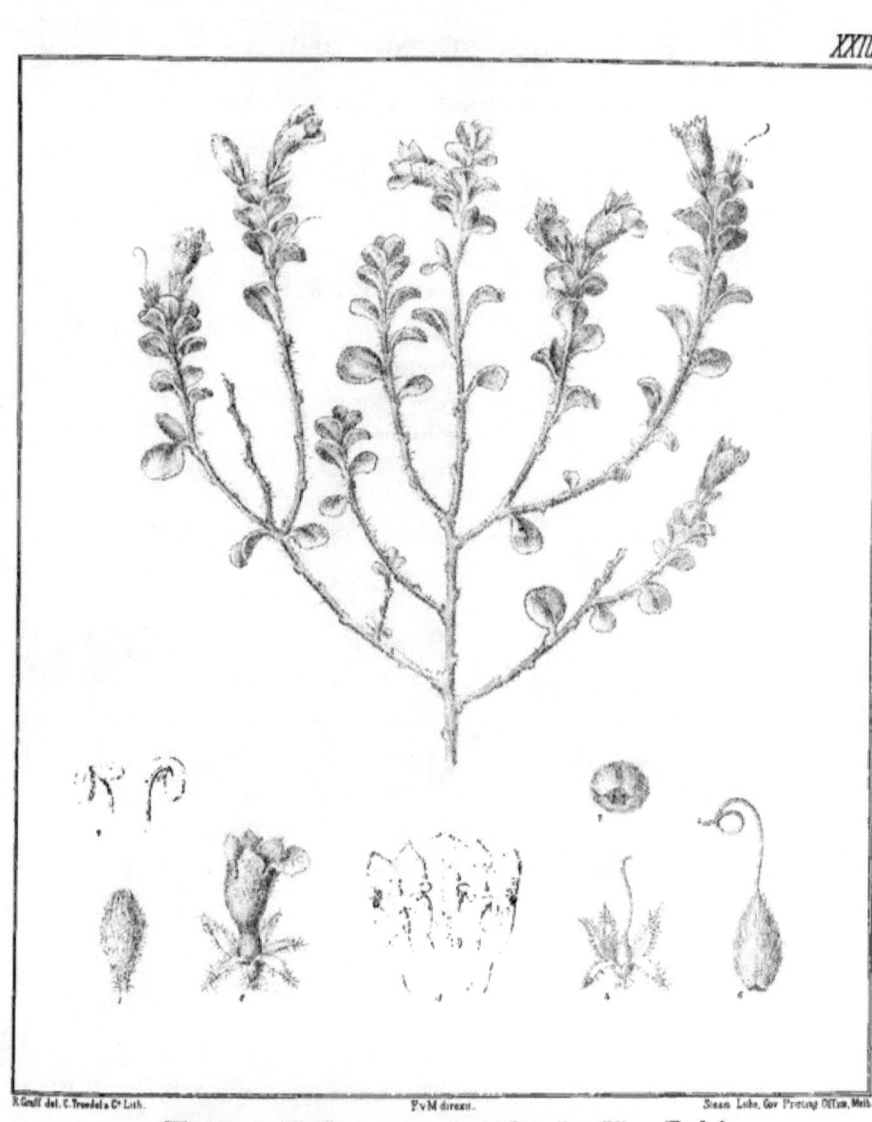

Eremophila strongylophylla *FvM.*

Eremophila oppositifolia.

R. Brown, Prodromus floræ Novæ Hollandiæ 518 (1810).

PLATE XXIV.

Figure 1, flower-bud.
    2, unexpanded flowers.
    3, expanded flower.
    4, corolla, laid open.
    5, stamens, front- and back-view.
    6, calyx with pistil.
    7, side-view of fruit.
    8, lower portion of fruit, seen from beneath.
    9, transverse section of fruit.
    10, longitudinal section of fruit.
    11, seeds.

        All more or less enlarged.

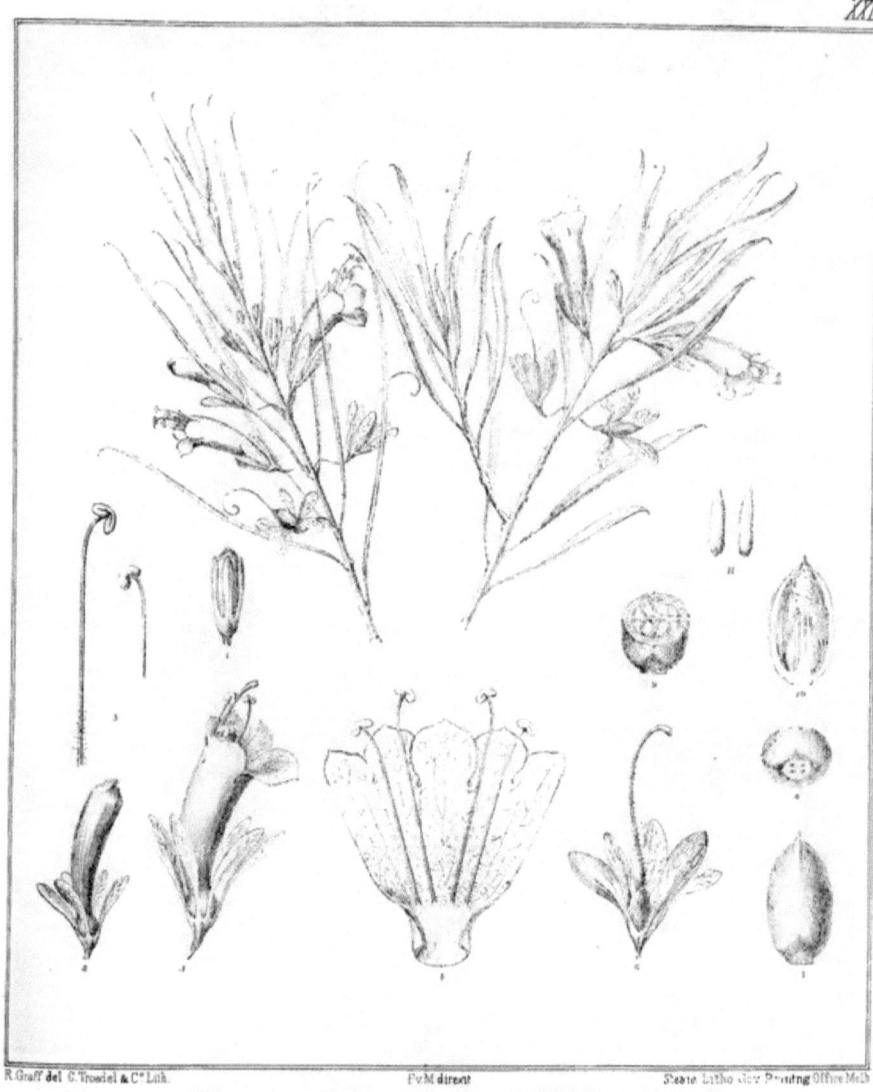

Eremophila oppositifolia R.Brown.

Eremophila Mitchelli.

Bentham in Mitchell's Tropical Australia 31 (1848).

PLATE XXV.

Figure 1, unexpanded flower.

    2, expanded flower.

    3, corolla, laid open.

    4, stamens, front- and back-view.

    5, pistil.

    6, side-view of fruit.

    7, lower portion of fruit, seen from beneath.

    8, transverse section of fruit.

    9, longitudinal section of fruit.

    10, seeds.

All enlarged, but to a different degree.

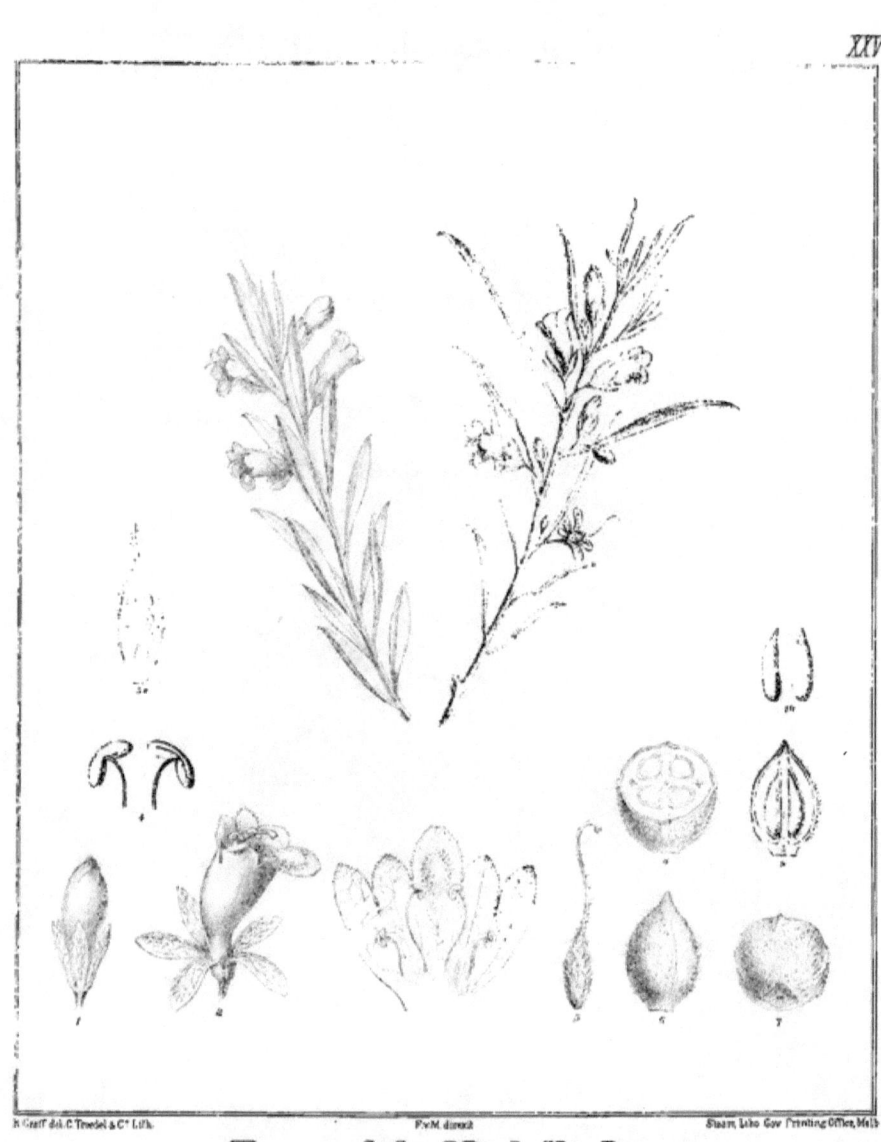

Eremophila Mitchelli BENTHAM.

Eremophila Paisleyi.

F. v. M. in Report on plants of Babbage's Expedition 17 (1858).

PLATE XXVI.

Figure 1, unexpanded flower.

2, expanded flower.

3, corolla, laid open.

4, stamens, front- and back-view.

5, calyx with pistil.

6, side-view of fruit.

7, transverse section of fruit.

8, longitudinal section of fruit.

All more or less enlarged.

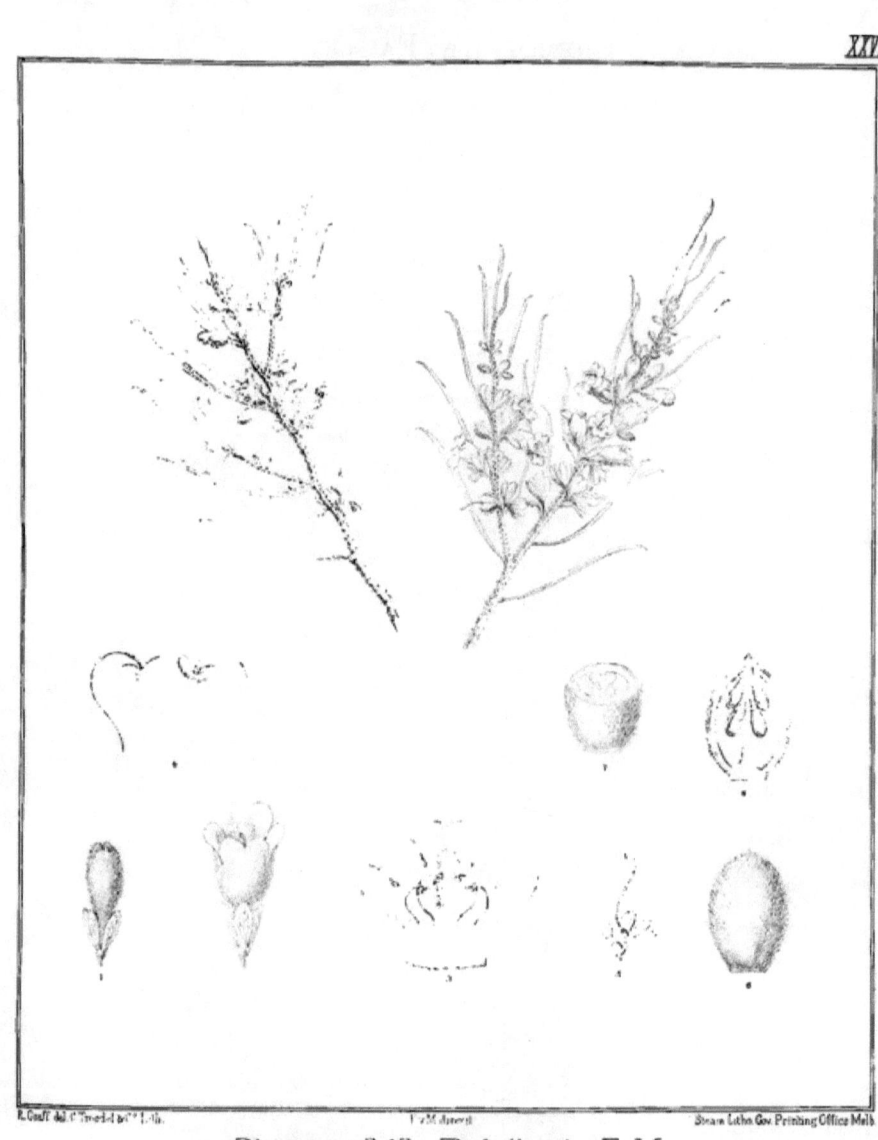

Eremophila Paisleyi *FvM*

Eremophila Sturtii.

R. Brown, Appendix to Sturt's Expedition 22 (1849).

PLATE XXVII.

Figure 1, unexpanded flower.

2, expanded flower.

3, corolla, laid open.

4, stamens, front- and back-view.

5, pistil.

6, side-view of fruit.

7, transverse section of fruit.

8, longitudinal section of fruit.

All more or less enlarged.

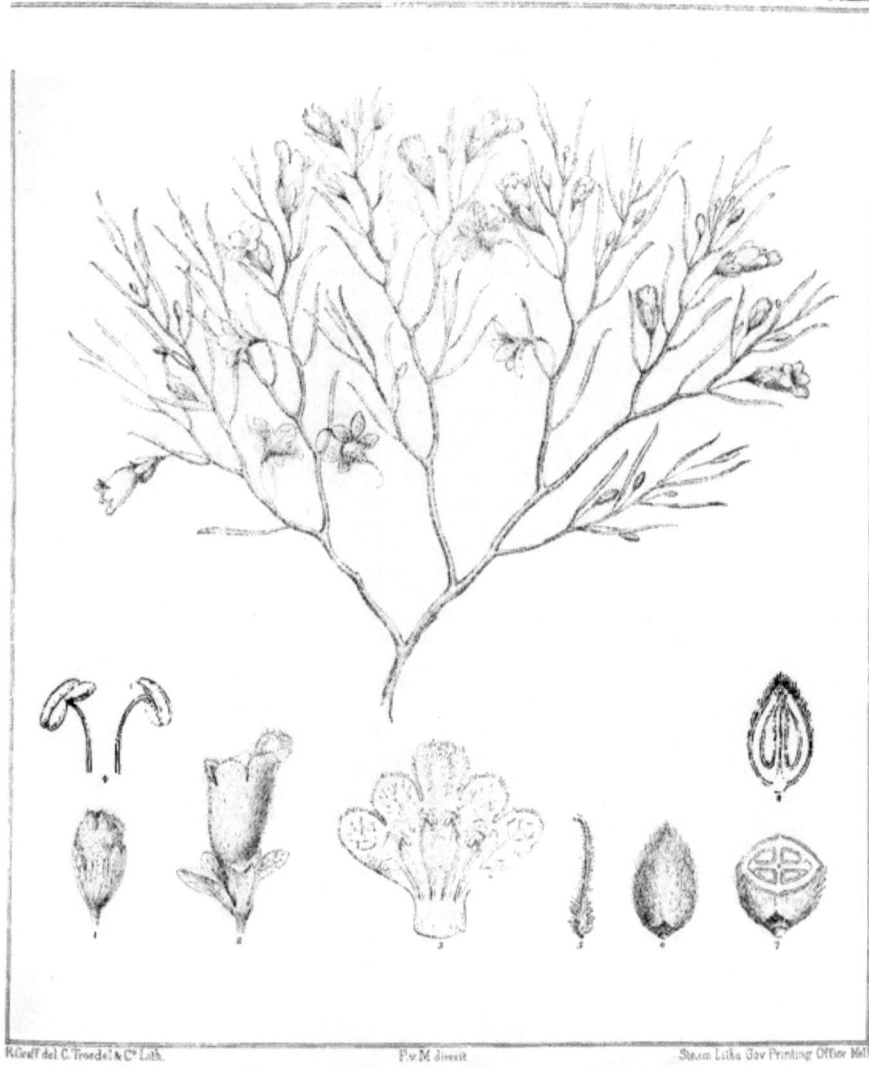

Eremophila Sturtii R.Brown.

Eremophila exilifolia.

F. v. M. Fragmenta phytographiæ Australiæ x. 88 (1876).

PLATE XXVIII.

Figure 1, unexpanded flower.

2, expanded flower.

3, corolla, laid open.

4, stamens, front- and back-view.

5, calyx with pistil.

6, side-view of fruit.

7, lower portion of fruit, seen from beneath

8, transverse section of fruit.

9, longitudinal section of fruit.

10, seeds.

All enlarged, but to a different degree.

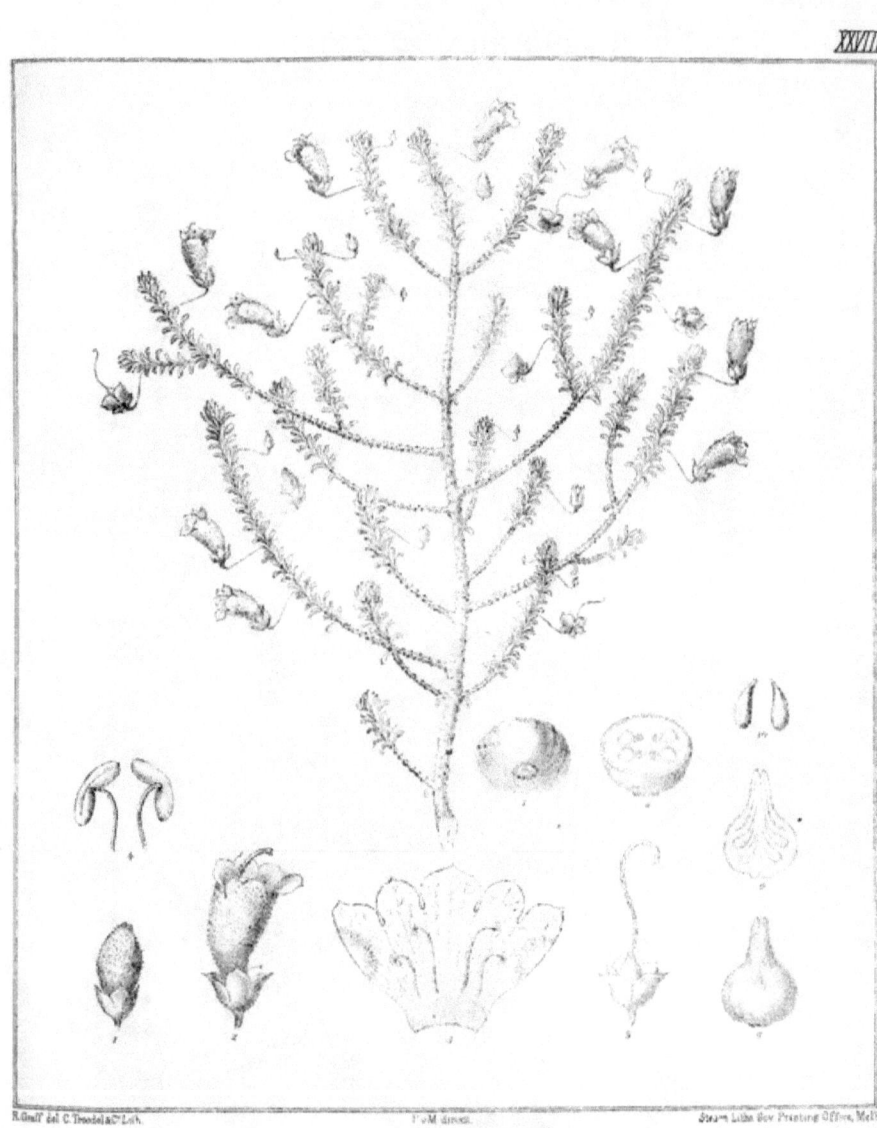

Eremophila exilifolia FvM.

Eremophila Gibsoni.

F v. M. Fragmenta phytographiæ Australiæ viii. 227 (1874).

PLATE XXIX.

Figure 1, a leaf.

    2, unexpanded flower.

    3, expanded flower.

    4, corolla, laid open.

    5, stamens, front- and back-view.

    6, calyx with pistil.

    7, side-view of fruit.

    8, transverse section of fruit.

    9, longitudinal section of fruit.

    10, seeds.

    All more or less enlarged.

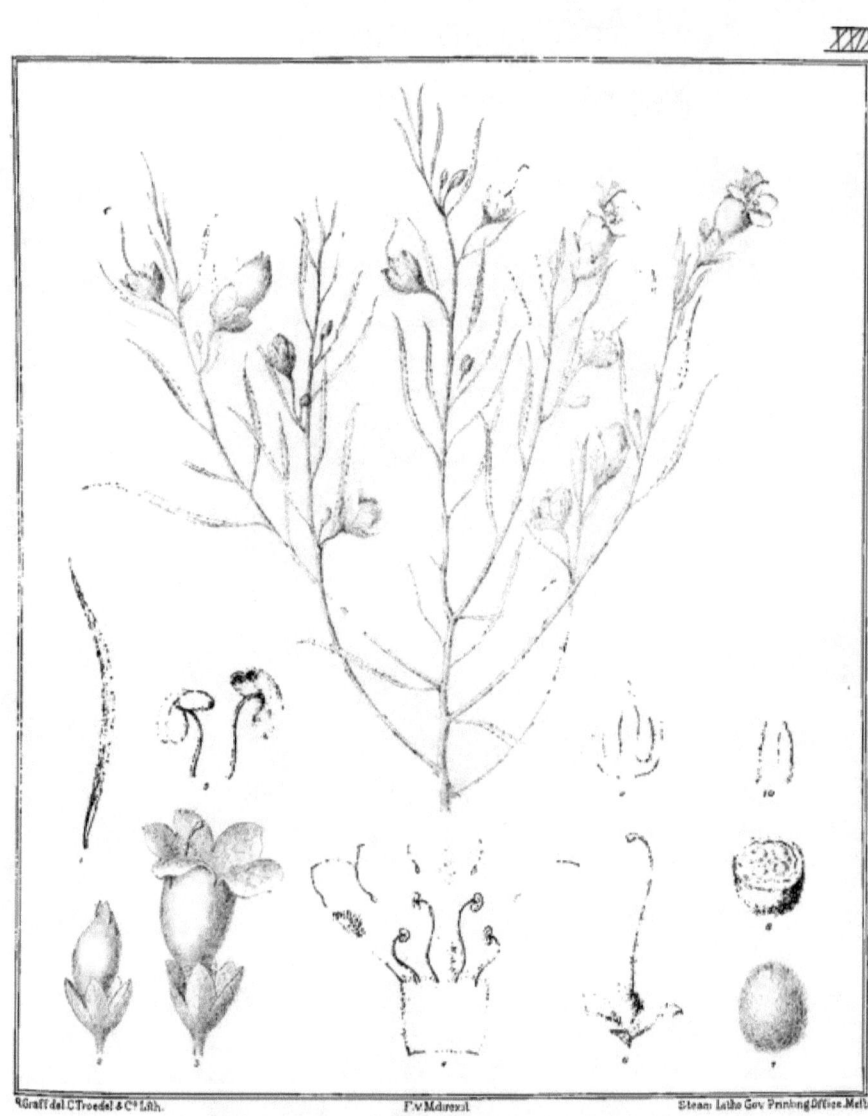

Eremophila Gibsoni F.vM.

Eremophila Clarkei.

F. v. M. Fragmenta phytographiæ Australiæ i. 208 (1859).

PLATE XXX.

Figure 1, unexpanded flower.

2, expanded flower.

3, corolla, laid open.

4, stamens, front- and back-view.

5, pistil.

6, side-view of fruit.

7, transverse section of fruit.

8, longitudinal section of fruit.

All more or less enlarged

Eremophila Clarkei *FvM*

Eremophila Latrobei.

F v. M. in Proceedings of the Royal Society of Tasmania iii. 294 (1858).

PLATE XXXI.

Figure 1, flower-bud.

2, expanded flower.

3, corolla, laid open.

4, stamens, front- and back-view.

5, calyx with pistil.

6, side-view of fruit.

7, lower portion of fruit, seen from beneath.

8, transverse section of fruit.

9, longitudinal section of fruit.

10, seeds.

All enlarged, but in various degree.

Eremophila Latrobei F.v.M.

Eremophila alternifolia.

R. Brown, Prodromus floræ Novæ Hollandiæ 518 (1810).

PLATE XXXII.

Figure 1, unexpanded flower.

2, expanded flower.

3, corolla, laid open.

4, stamens, front- and back-view.

5, pistil.

6, side-view of fruit.

7, lower portion of fruit, seen from beneath.

8, transverse section of fruit.

9, longitudinal section of fruit.

10, seeds.

All enlarged, but in various degree.

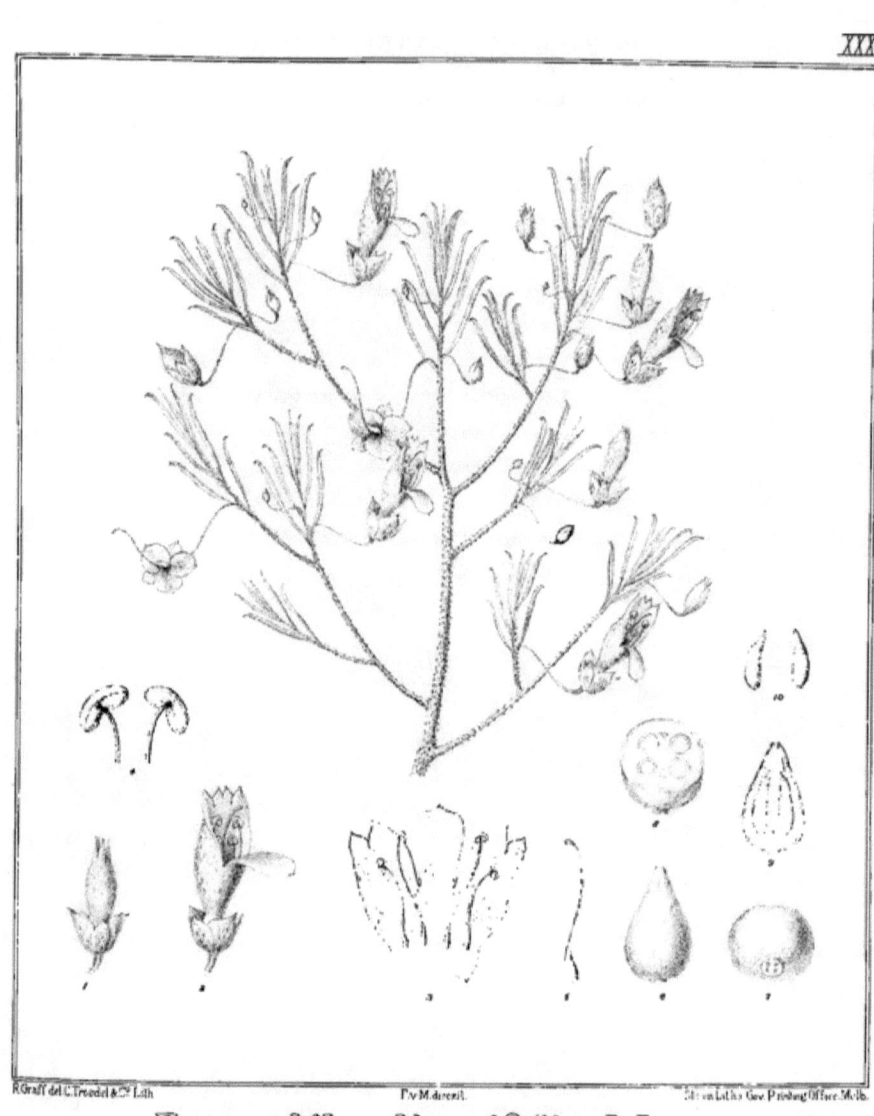

Eremophila alternifolia R. Brown.

Eremophila latifolia.

F. v. M. in Schlechtendal's Linnæa xxv. 428 (1852).

PLATE XXXIII.

Figure 1, flower in bud.

2, expanded flower.

3, corolla, laid open.

4, stamens, front- and back-view.

5, pistil.

6, side-view of fruit.

7, transverse section of fruit.

8, longitudinal section of fruit.

9, seeds.

All enlarged, but to a various degree.

Eremophila latifolia. F.vM

Eremophila denticulata.

F. v. M. Fragmenta phytographiæ Australiæ i. 125 (1859).

PLATE XXXIV.

Figure 1, unexpanded flower.

    2, expanded flower.

    3, corolla, laid open.

    4, stamens, front- and back-view.

    5, calyx with pistil.

    6, fruit, portion of the outer layer of the pericarp removed.

    7, fruit, the whole outer layer of the pericarp removed.

    8, transverse section of fruit.

    9, longitudinal section of fruit.

    10, seeds.

        All enlarged, but in various degree.

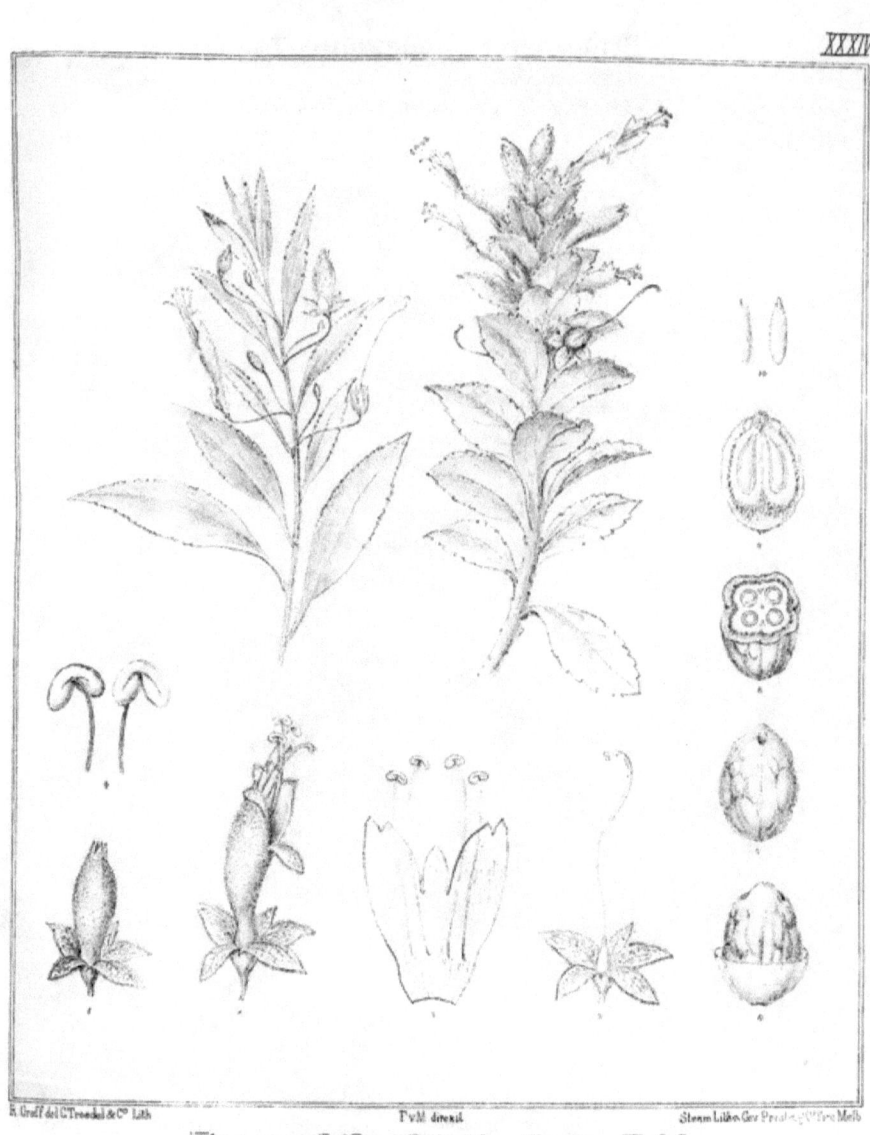

Eremophila denticulata F.vM

Eremophila maculata.

F. v. M. in Proceedings of the Royal Society of Tasmania iii. 297 (1858).

PLATE XXXV.

Figure 1, flower in bud.

2, unexpanded flowers.

3, expanded flower.

4, corolla, laid open.

5, stamens, front- and back-view.

6, pollen-grains.

7, calyx with pistil.

8, fruit with style adhering, side-view.

9, fruit, seen from beneath.

10, fruit without the outer layer of the pericarp.

11, transverse section of fruit.

12, longitudinal section of fruit.

13, seeds.

All enlarged, but in various degree.

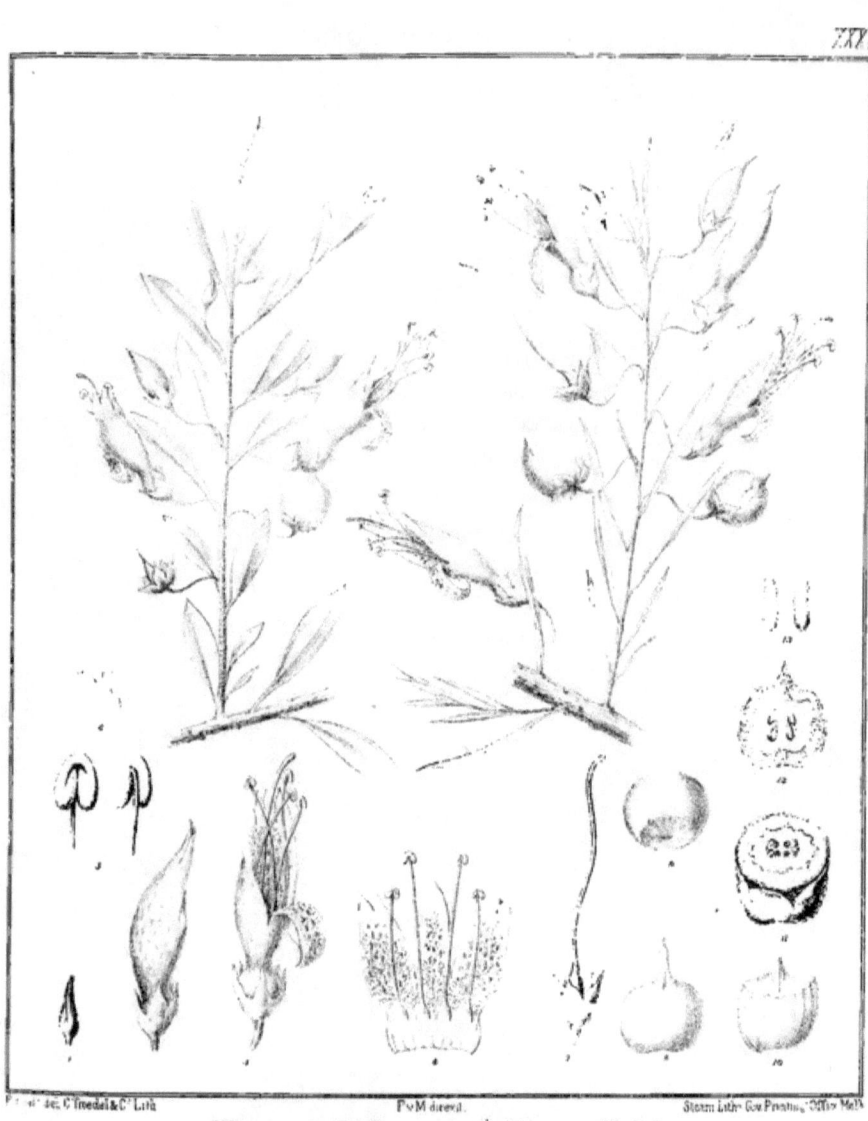

Eremophila maculata F.v.M

EREMOPHILA DUTTONI.

F. v. M. Report on Plants of Babbage's Expedition 16 (1858).

PLATE XXXVI.

Figure 1, flower, in bud.

2, expanded flower.

3, corolla, laid open.

4, stamens, front- and back-view.

5, pistil.

6, fruit, portion of the outer layer of the pericarp removed.

7, fruit without the outer layer of the pericarp.

8, transverse section of fruit.

9, longitudinal section of fruit.

10, seeds.

All enlarged, but in various degree.

Eremophila Duttoni FvM.

Eremophila Oldfieldi.

F. v. M. Fragmenta phytographiæ Australiæ i. 208 (1859).

PLATE XXXVII.

Figure 1, unexpanded flower.

    2, expanded flower.

    3, corolla, laid open.

    4, stamens, front- and back-view.

    5, calyx with pistil.

    6, side-view of fruit.

    7, lower portion of fruit, seen from beneath.

    8, transverse section of fruit.

    9, longitudinal section of fruit.

    10, seeds.

        All enlarged, but in various degree.

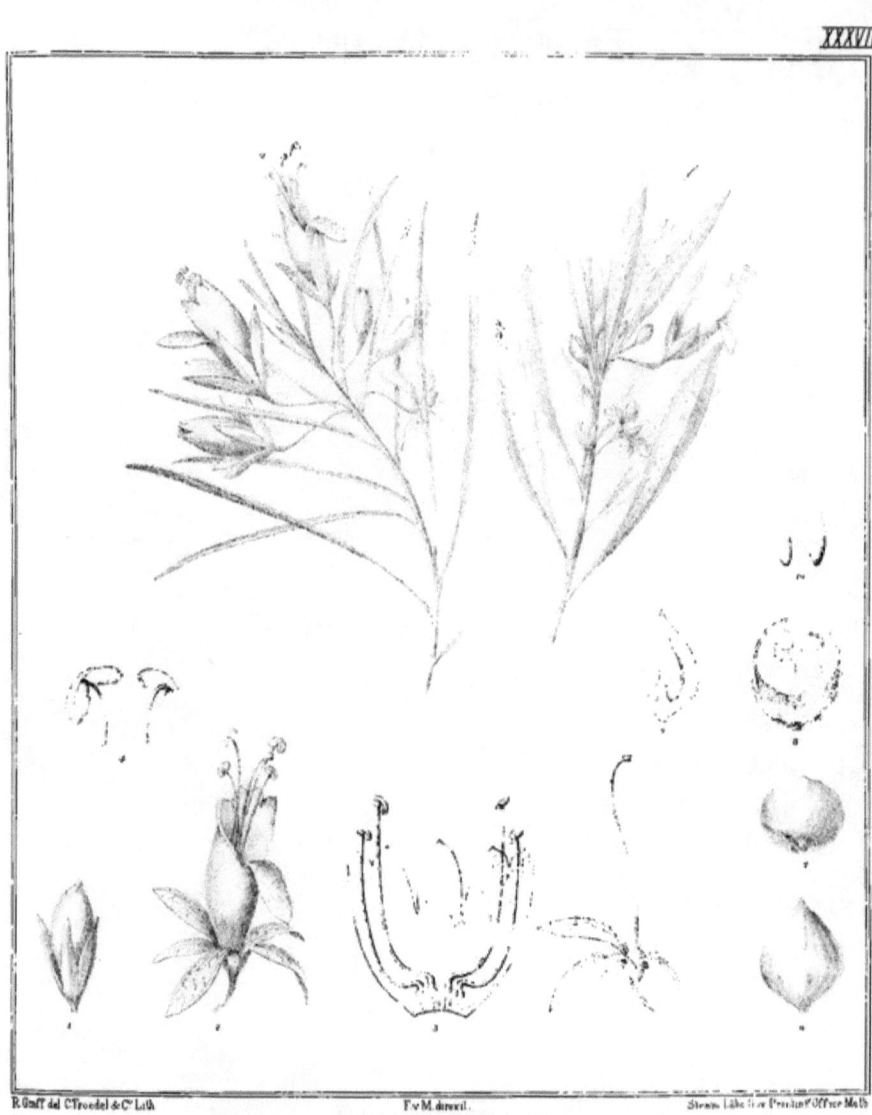

Eremophila Oldfieldi FvM

Eremophila Brownii.

F. v. M. in Proceedings of the Royal Society of Tasmania iii. 297 (1858).

PLATE XXXVIII.

Figure 1, unexpanded flower.

2, expanded flower.

3, corolla, laid open.

4, stamens, front- and back-view.

5, calyx with pistil.

6, fruit-bearing calyx.

7, side-view of fruit, the outer layer of the pericarp removed.

8, lower half of fruit, seen from beneath.

9, transverse section of fruit.

10, longitudinal section of fruit.

11, seeds.

All enlarged, but in various degree.

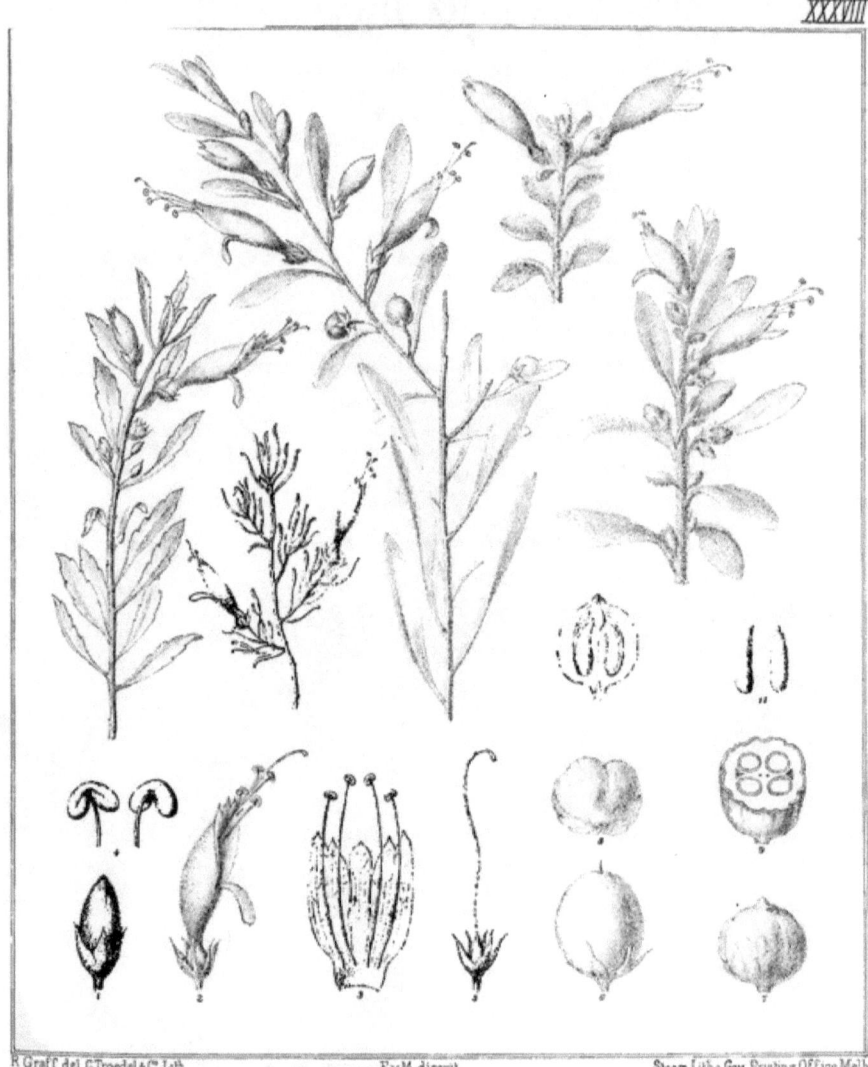

Eremophila Brownii F.v.M.

Eremophila Youngii.

F. v. M. Fragmenta phytographiæ Australiæ x. 16 (1876)

PLATE XXXIX.

Figure 1, flower in early bud.

2, unexpanded flowers.

3, expanded flower.

4, corolla, laid open.

5, stamens, front- and back-view.

6, calyx with pistil.

7, side-view of fruit.

8, lower half of fruit, seen from beneath.

9, transverse section of fruit.

10, longitudinal section of fruit.

11, seeds.

All enlarged, but in various degree.

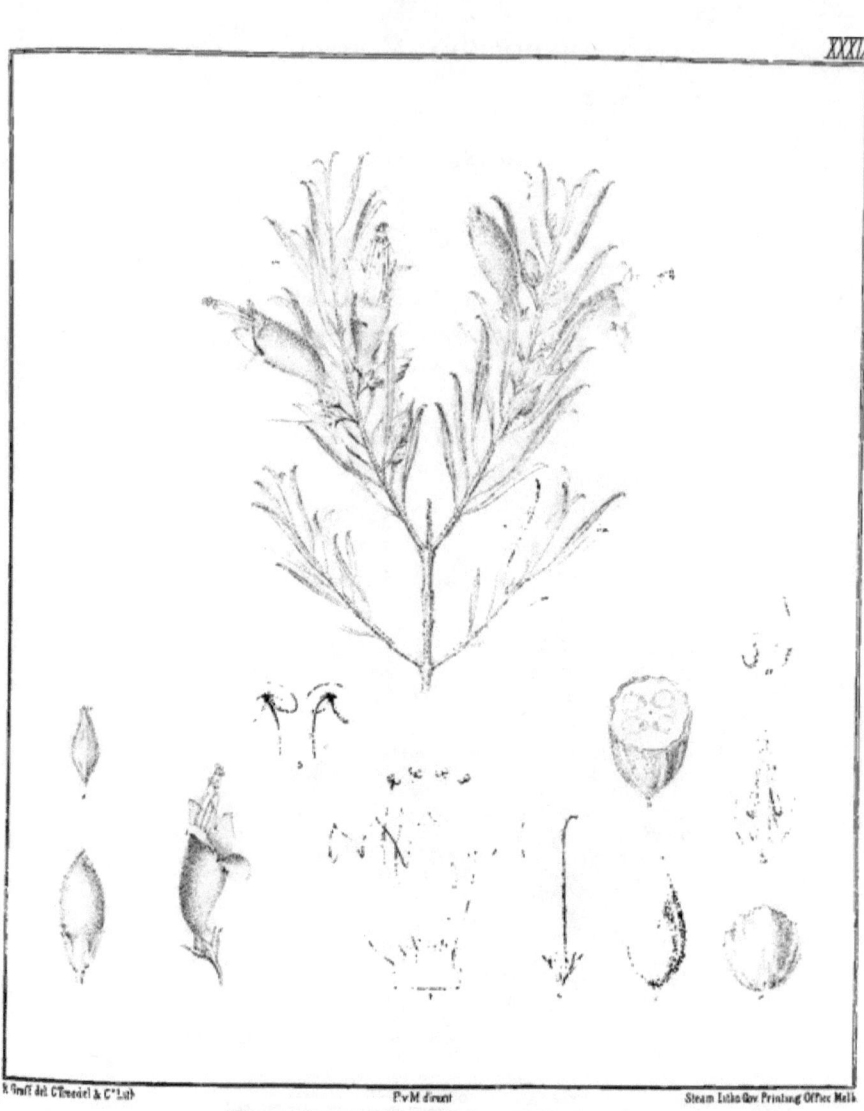

Eremophila Youngii. F.v.M.

Eremophila scoparia.

F. v. M. in Proceedings of the Royal Society of Tasmania iii. 296 (1858).

PLATE XL.

Figure 1, young branchlet.
2, flower-bud in early stage.
3, unexpanded flower, young.
4, expanded flower.
5, corolla, laid open.
6, stamens, front- and back-view.
7, pistil.
8, side-view of fruit.
9, lower portion of fruit, seen from beneath.
10, transverse section of two fruits.
11, longitudinal section of a fruit.
12, seeds.

All enlarged, but in various degree.

Eremophila scoparia F.v.M.

Eremophila Dalyana.

F. v. M. Fragmenta phytographiæ Australiæ v. 22 (1865).

PLATE XLI.

Figure 1, portion of branchlet.

    2, portion of a leaf.

    3, flower in bud.

    4 and 5, unexpanded flowers.

    6, expanded flower.

    7, corolla, laid open.

    8, stamens, front- and back-view.

    9, calyx with pistil.

    10, side-view of fruit.

    11, lower half of fruit, seen from beneath.

    12, transverse section of fruit.

    13, longitudinal section of fruit.

        All enlarged, but in various degree.

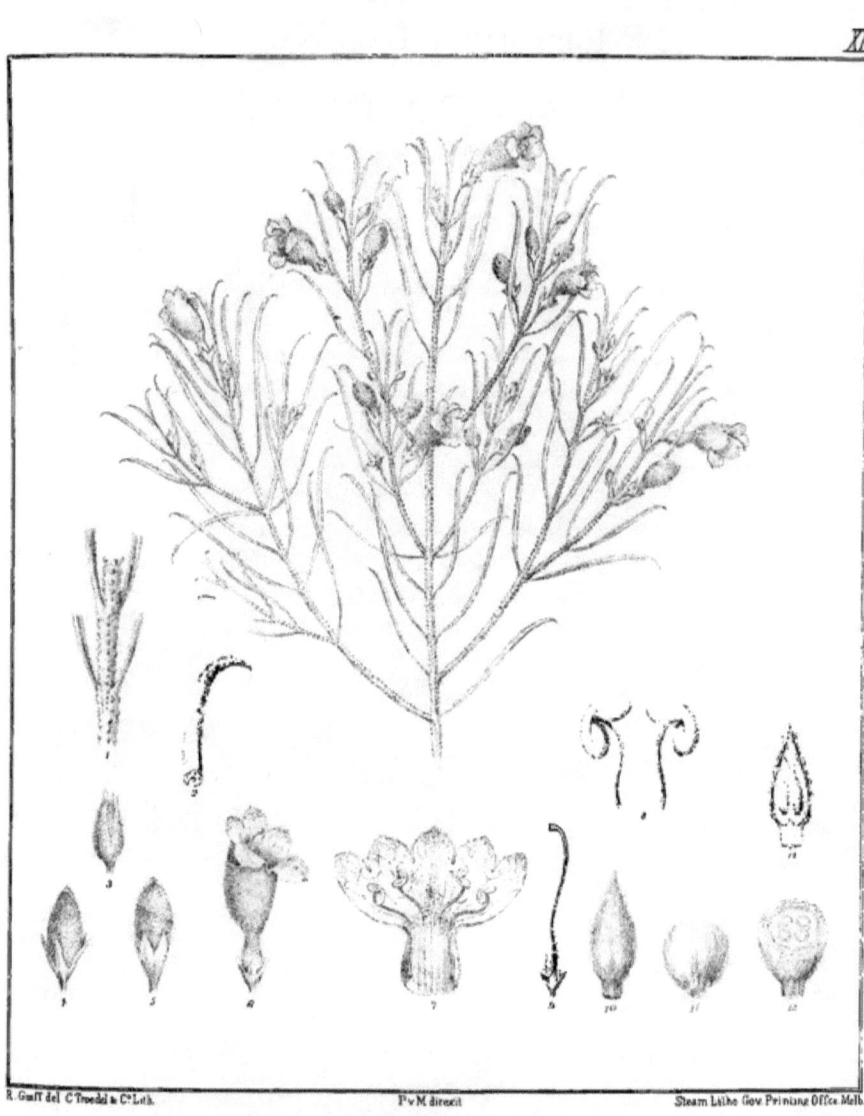

Eremophila Dalyana. F.v.M.

Eremophila Pantoni.

F. v. M. in Wing's Southern Science Record ii. 251 (1882).

PLATE XLII.

Figure 1, portion of branchlet.

2, branched hairs of vestiture.

3, flower-bud.

4, unexpanded flower.

5, expanded flower.

6, corolla, laid open.

7, stamens, front- and back-view.

8, pistil.

9, side-view of fruit.

10, lower half of fruit, seen from beneath.

11, transverse section of fruit.

12, longitudinal section of fruit.

13, seeds.

All enlarged, but in various degree.

Eremophila Pantoni F v M

Eremophila Delisserii.

F. v. M. Fragmenta phytographiæ Australiæ v. 108 t. 42 (1865).

PLATE XLIII.

Figure 1, star-hairs of vestiture.

    2, flower-bud.

    3, unexpanded flower.

    4, expanded flower.

    5, corolla, laid open.

    6, stamens, front- and back-view.

    7, pistil.

    8, side-view of fruit.

    9, lower half of fruit, seen from beneath.

    10, aged calyx.

    11, transverse section of fruit.

    12, longitudinal section of fruit.

All enlarged, but in various degree.

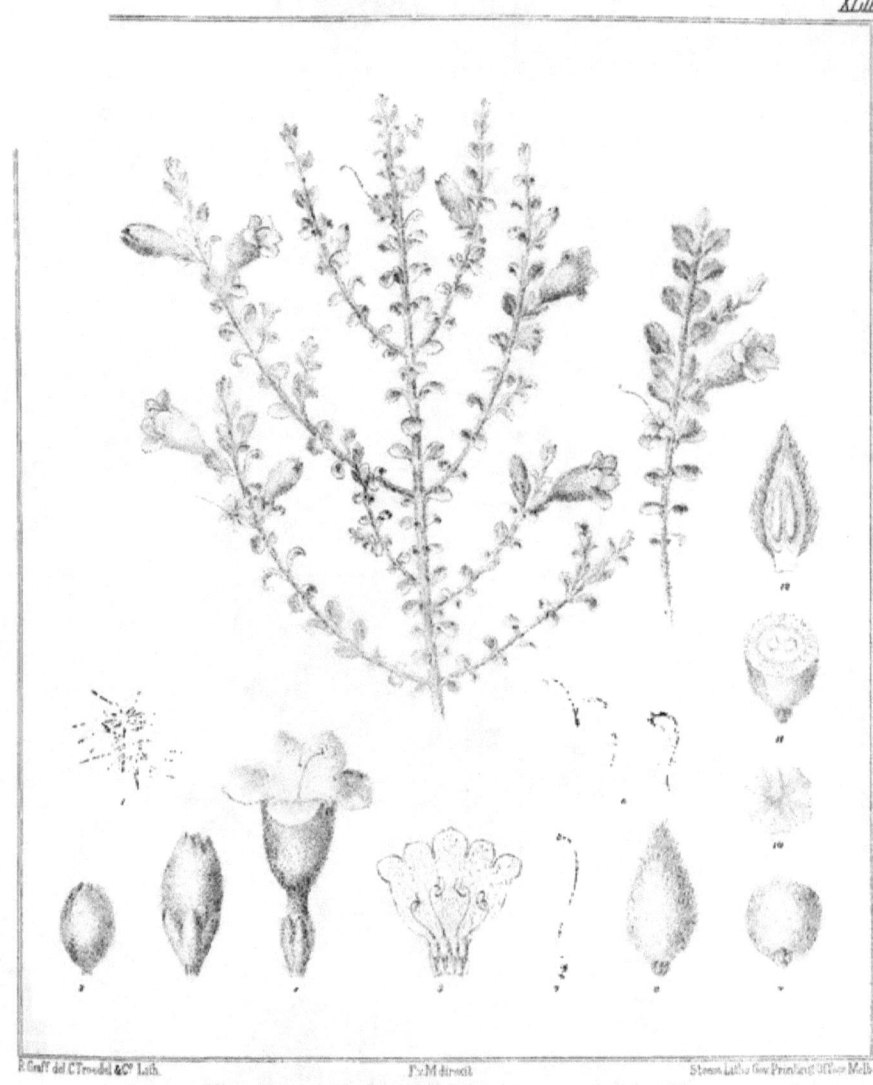

Eremophila Delisserii FvM

Eremophila Behriana.

F. v. M. in Proceedings of the Royal Society of Tasmania iii. 296 (1858).

PLATE XLIV.

Figure 1, leaf.

2, unexpanded flower.

3, expanded flower.

4, corolla, laid open.

5, stamens, front- and back-view.

6, calyx with pistil.

7, side-view of fruit.

8, transverse section of fruit.

9, longitudinal section of fruit.

All enlarged, but in various degree.

Eremophila Behriana F.vM.

Eremophila brevifolia.

F. v. M. Systematic Census of Australian plants 104 (1882).

PLATE XLV.

Figure 1, leaf.
    2, flower-bud.
    3, expanded flower.
    4, corolla, laid open.
    5, stamens, front- and back-view.
    6, pistil.
    7, side-view of fruit.
    8, lower half of fruit, seen from beneath.
    9, transverse section of fruit.
    10, longitudinal section of fruit.
    11, seeds.

    All enlarged, but in various degree.

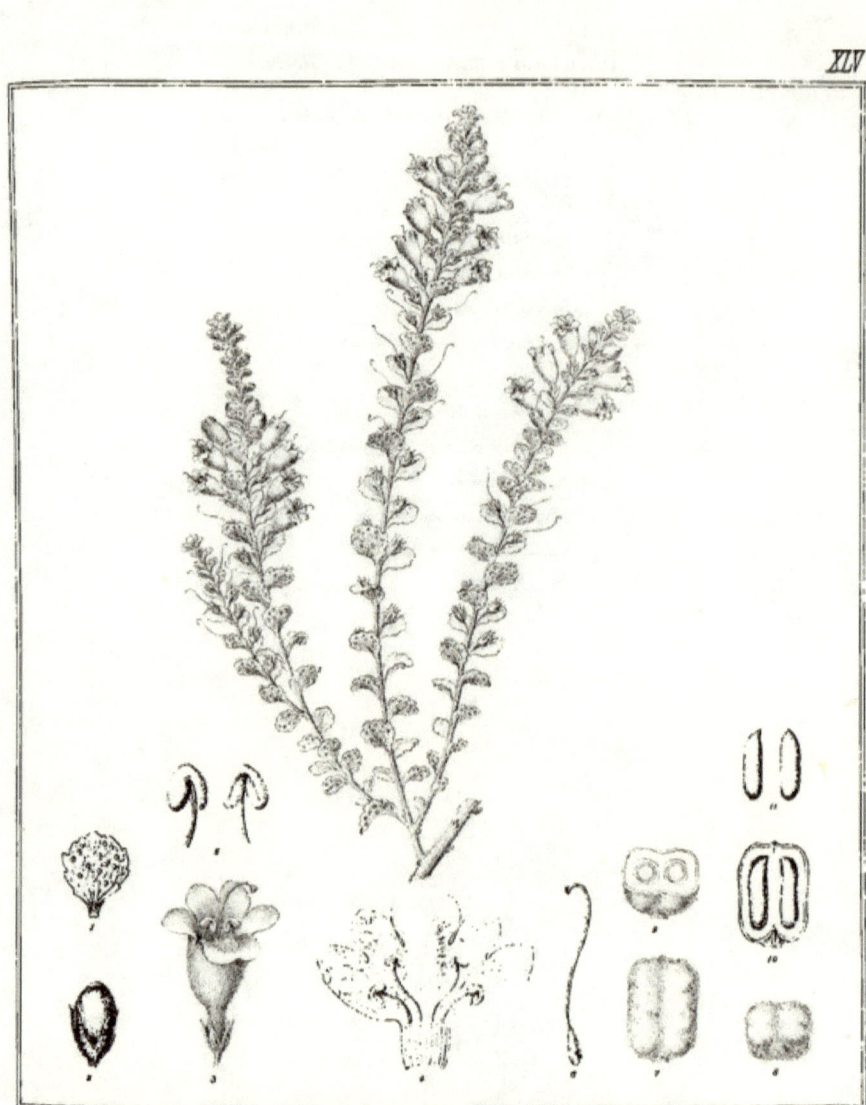

Eremophila brevifolia F.vM.

EREMOPHILA CRASSIFOLIA.

F. v. M. in Proceedings of the Royal Society of Tasmania iii. 297 (1858).

PLATE XLVI.

Figures 1 and 2, unexpanded flowers.

3, expanded flower.

4, corolla, laid open.

5, stamens, front- and back-view.

6, pistil.

7, fruit, side-view.

8, lower portion of fruit, seen from beneath.

9, transverse section of fruit.

10, longitudinal section of fruit.

11, seeds.

All enlarged, but in various degree.

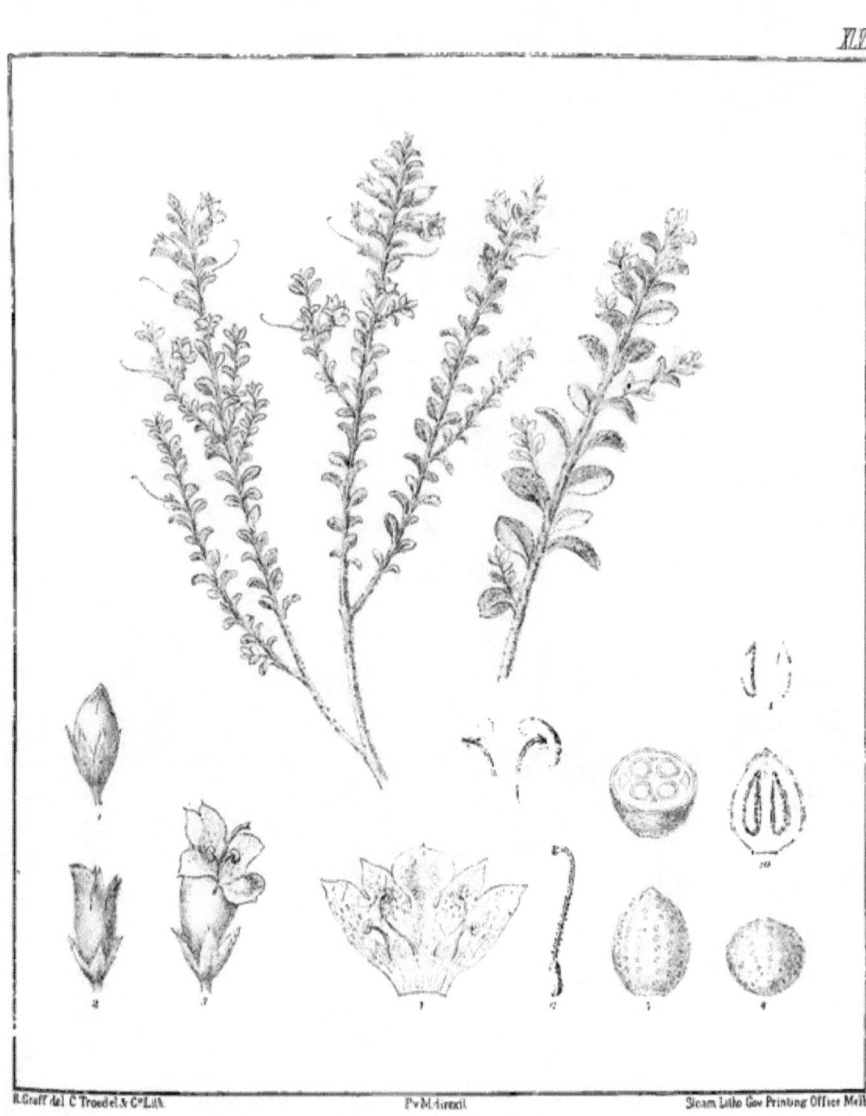

Eremophila crassifolia. F.v.M.

Eremophila Woollsiana.

F. v. M. Fragmenta phytographiæ Australiæ i. 125, t. 7 (1859).

PLATE XLVII.

Figure 1, flower in bud.
2, expanded flower.
3, corolla, laid open.
4, stamens, front- and back-view.
5, calyx with pistil.
6, side-view of fruit.
7, lower portion of fruit, seen from beneath.
8, transverse section of fruit.
9, longitudinal section of fruit.
10, seeds.

All enlarged, but in various degree.

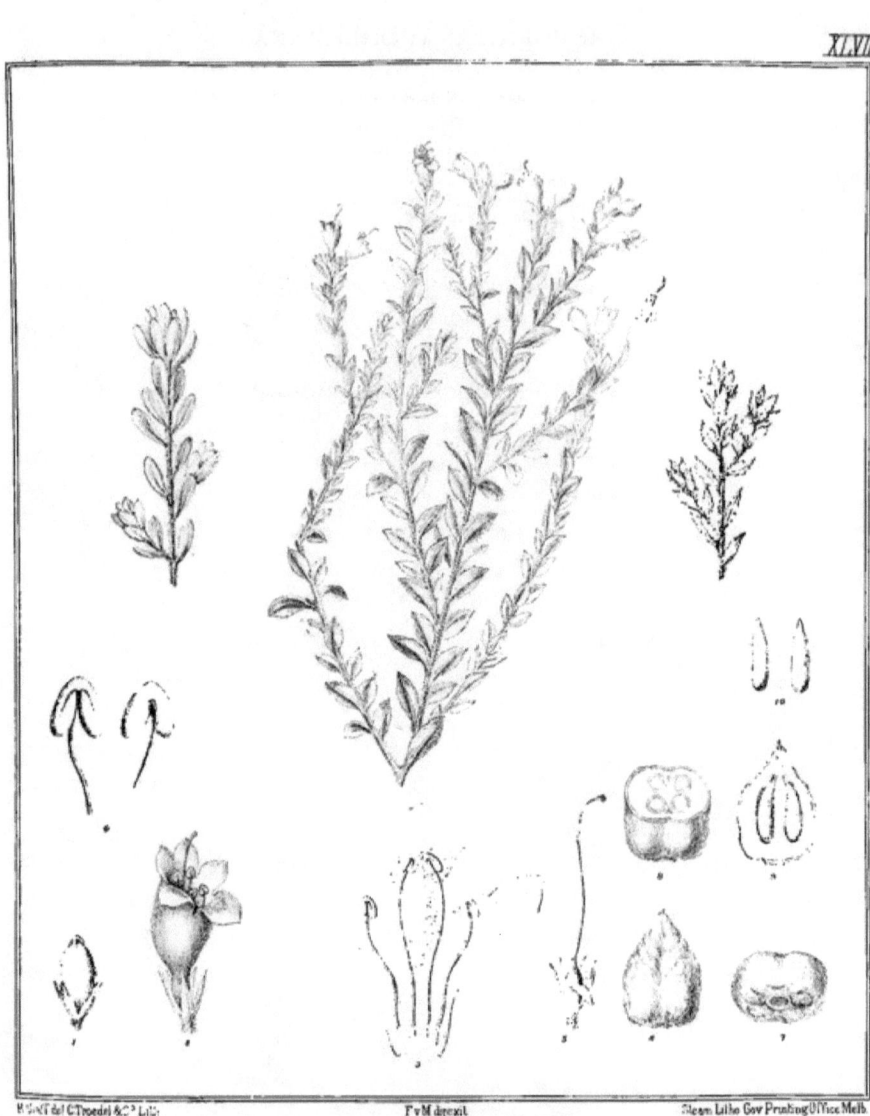

Eremophila Woollsiana FvM

Eremophila microtheca.

F. v. M. in Bentham's Flora Australiensis v. 14 (1870).

PLATE XLVIII.

Figure 1, branched hair of vestiture.

2, flower in bud.

3, expanded flower.

4, corolla, laid open.

5, stamens, front- and back-view.

6, pistil.

7, side-view of fruit.

8, fruit, seen from beneath.

9, transverse section of fruit.

10, longitudinal section of fruit.

11, seeds.

All enlarged, but in various degree.

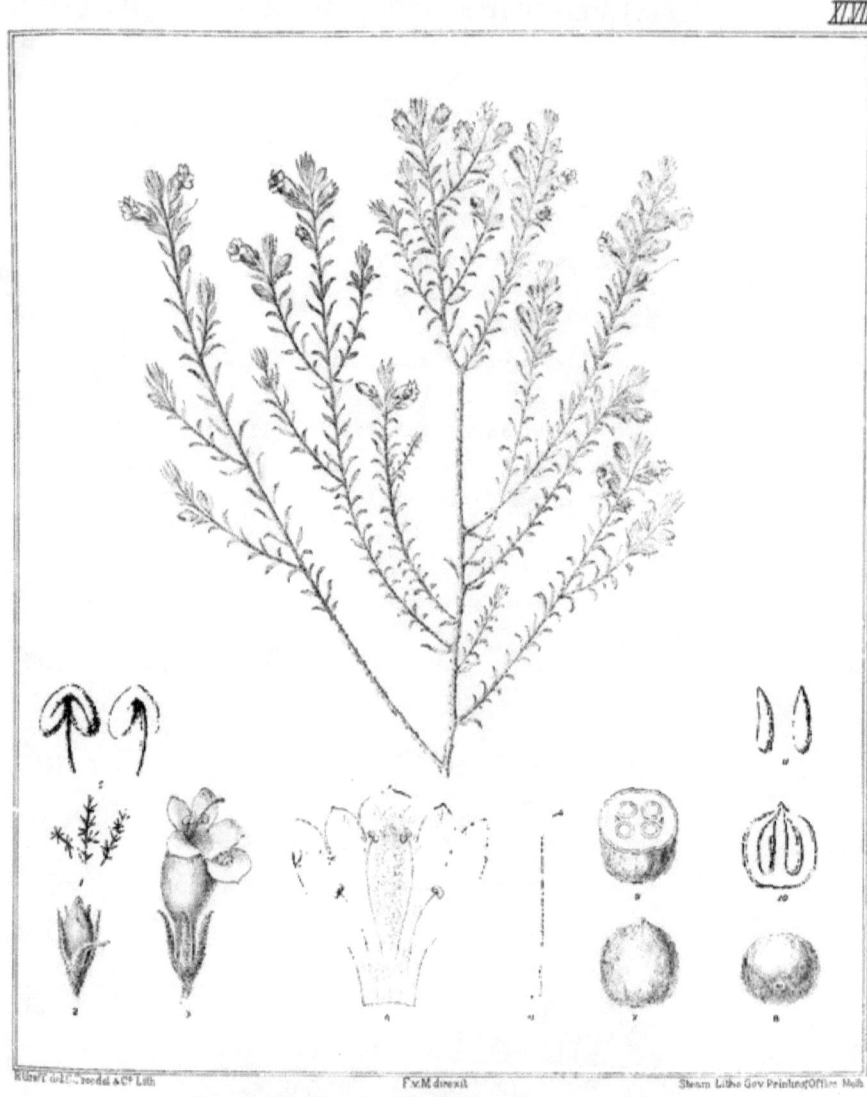

Eremophila microtheca FvM

Eremophila densifolia.

F. v. M. Fragmenta phytographiæ Australiæ ii. 160 (1861).

PLATE XLIX.

Figure 1, a leaf.

    2, branched hairs.

    3, unexpanded flower.

    4, expanded flower.

    5, corolla, laid open.

    6, calyx with pistil.

    7, side-view of fruit.

    8, lower half of fruit, seen from beneath.

    9, transverse section of fruit.

    10, longitudinal section of fruit.

    11, seeds.

All enlarged, but in various degree.

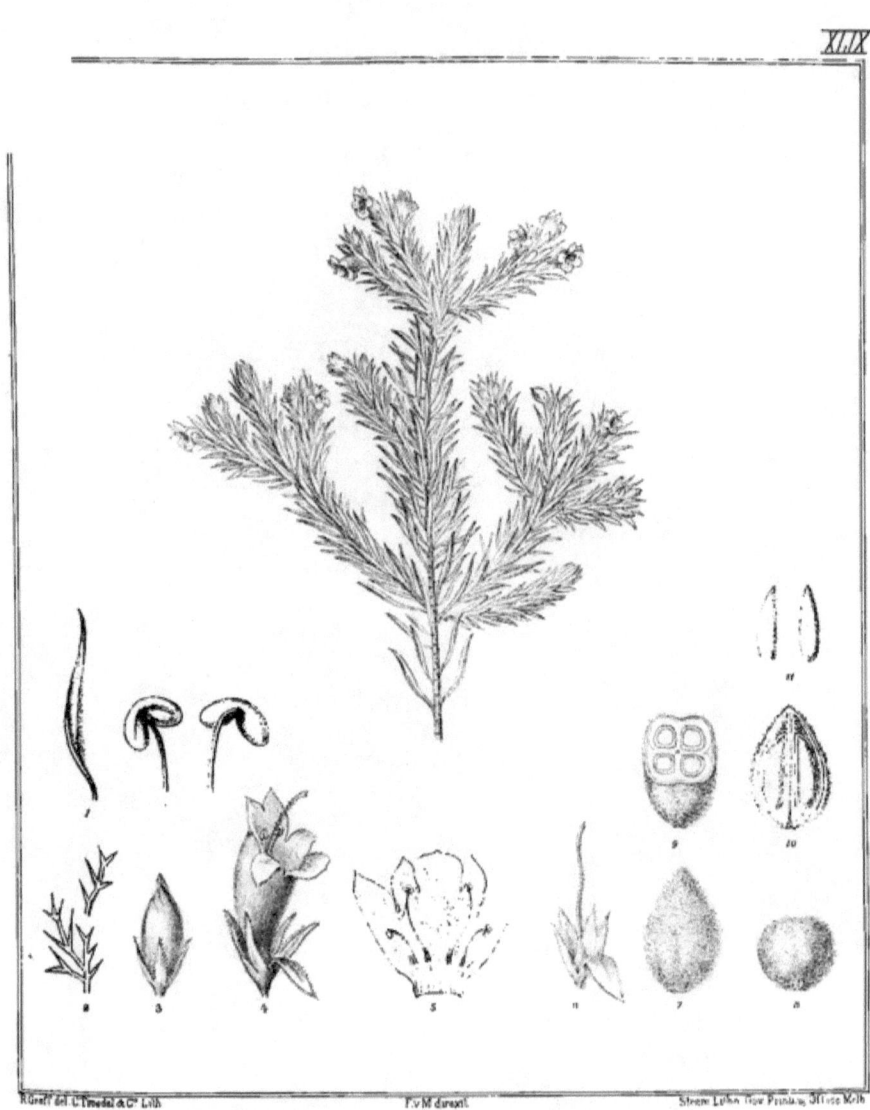

Eremophila densifolia FvM.

Eremophila Weldii.

F. v. M. Fragmenta phytographiæ Australiæ vii. 109 (1870).

PLATE L.

Figure 1, unexpanded flower.

2, expanded flower.

3, corolla, laid open.

4, stamens.

5, calyx with pistil.

6, side-view of fruit.

7, lower portion of fruit, seen from beneath.

8, transverse section of fruit.

9, longitudinal section of fruit.

10, seeds.

All enlarged, but in various degree.

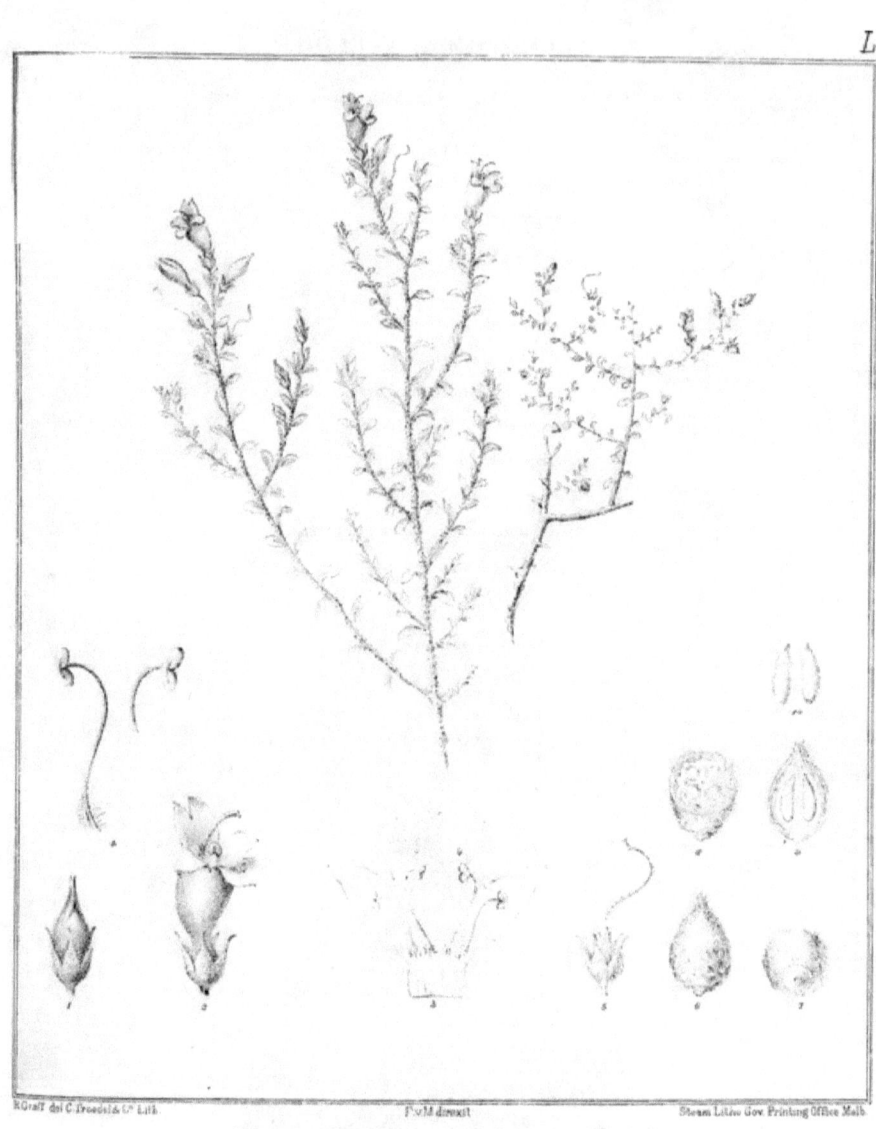

Eremophila Weldii FvM.

Eremophila Dempsteri.

F. v. M. Fragmenta phytographiæ Australiæ x. 60 (1876).

PLATE LI.

Figure 1, flower-bud.

2, unexpanded flower.

3, expanded flower.

4, corolla, laid open.

5, stamens, front- and back-view.

6, calyx with pistil.

7, side-view of fruit.

8, lower portion of fruit, seen from beneath.

9, transverse section of fruit.

10, longitudinal section of fruit.

11, seeds.

All enlarged, but in various degree.

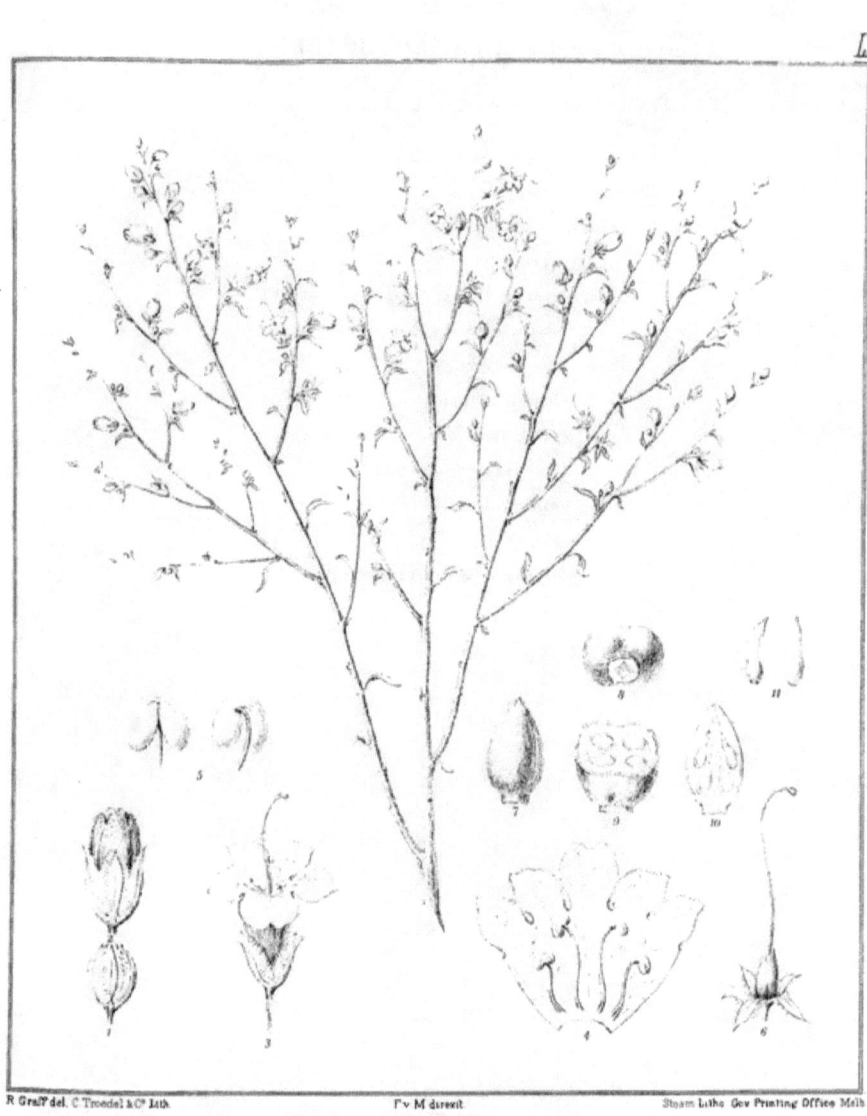

Eremophila Dempsteri F.v.M.

Eremophila gibbosifolia.

F. v. M. in Report on plants of Babbage's Expedition 18 (1858).

PLATE LII.

Figure 1, different leaves, front-, side- and back-views.

    2, unexpanded flower.

    3, expanded flower.

    4, corolla, laid open.

    5, stamens, front- and back-view.

    6, calyx with pistil.

    7, side-view of fruit.

    8, lower portion of fruit, seen from beneath.

    9, transverse section of fruit.

    10, longitudinal section of fruit.

    11, seeds.

      All enlarged, but in various degree.

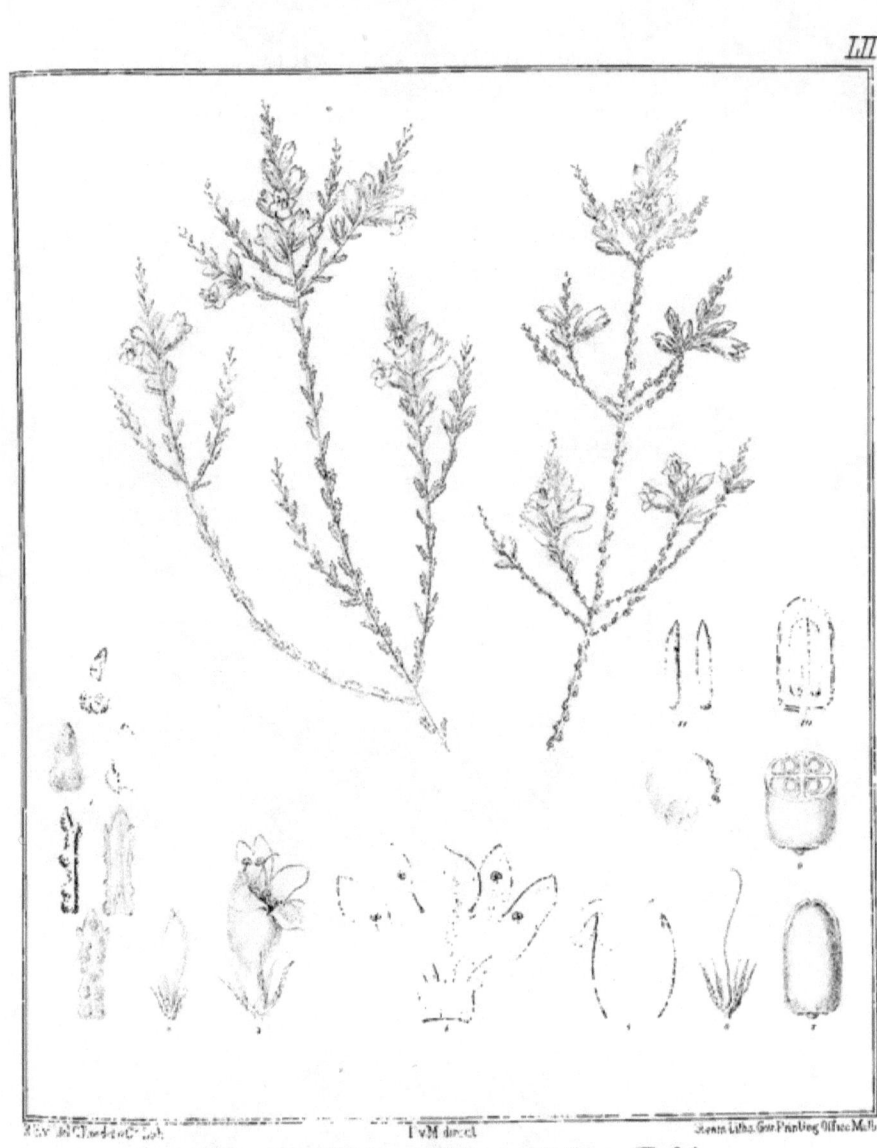

Eremophila gibbosifolia FvM

Eremophila adenotricha.

F. v. M. in Bentham's Flora Australiensis v. 15 (1870).

PLATE LIII.

Figure 1, glandular hairs of the general vestiture.

2, unexpanded flower.

3, expanded flower.

4, corolla, laid open.

5, stamens, front- and back-view.

6, calyx with pistil.

7, side-view of fruit.

8, the same, the outer layer of the pericarp removed.

9, lower portion of fruit, seen from beneath.

10, transverse section of fruit.

11, longitudinal section of fruit.

12, seeds.

All enlarged, but in various degree.

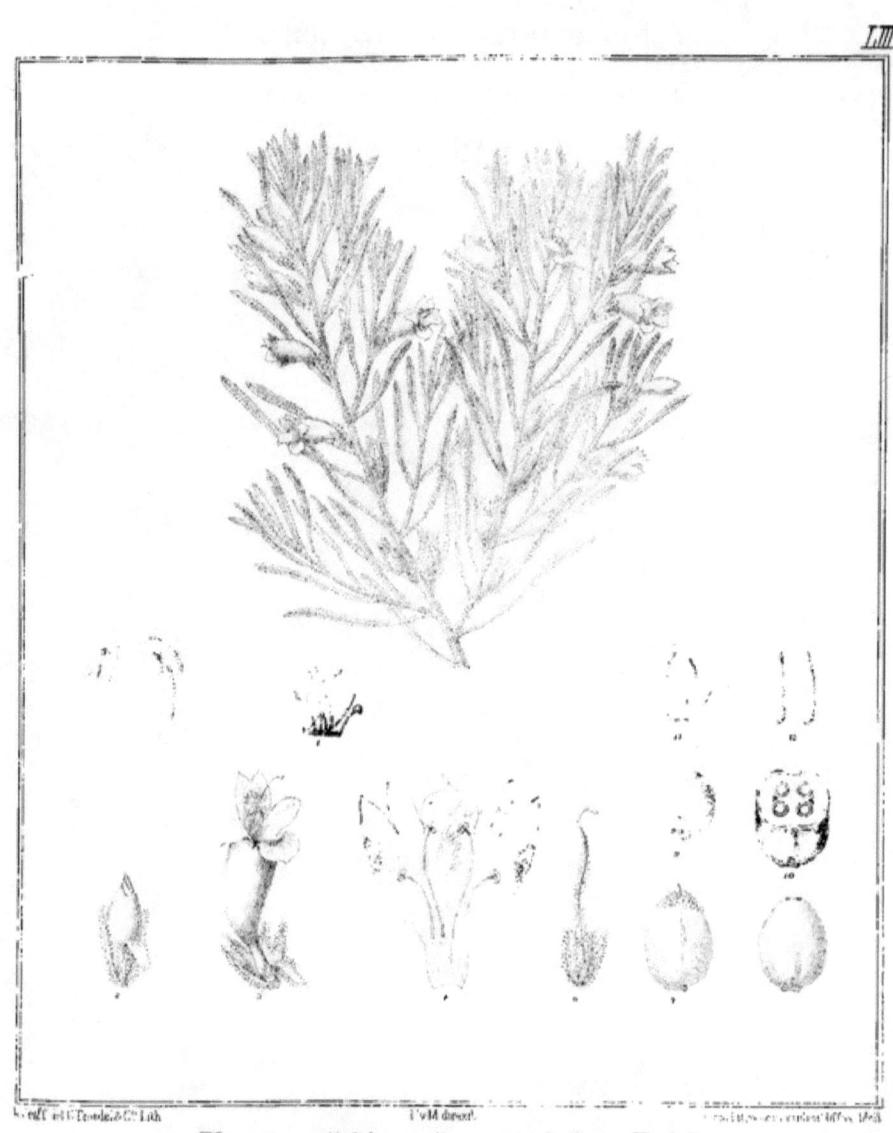

Eremophila adenotricha FvM

Eremophila Behriana.

F. v. M. in Proceedings of the Royal Society of Tasmania iii. 296 (1858).

PLATE XLIV.

Figure 1, leaf.

    2, unexpanded flower.

    3, expanded flower.

    4, corolla, laid open.

    5, stamens, front- and back-view.

    6, calyx with pistil.

    7, side-view of fruit.

    8, transverse section of fruit.

    9, longitudinal section of fruit.

All enlarged, but in various degree.

Eremophila Behriana FvM.

Eremophila divaricata.

F. v. M. in Proceedings of the Royal Society of Tasmania iii. 293 (1858).

PLATE LV.

Figure 1, flower-bud.

    2, unexpanded flower.

    3, expanded flower.

    4, corolla, laid open.

    5, stamens, front- and back-view, one with basal beard.

    6, calyx with pistil.

    7, fruit with calyx, side-view.

    8, the same, seen from beneath.

    9, transverse section of fruit.

    10, longitudinal section of fruit.

    11, seeds.

        All enlarged, but in various degree.

Eremophila divaricata FvM

Myoporum salsoloides.

Turczaninow in Bulletin de la Société Impériale des Naturalistes de Moscou xxxvi. 226 (1863).

PLATE LVI.

Figure 1, portion of branchlet with leaves.

2, unexpanded flower.

3, expanded flower.

4, corolla, laid open.

5, stamens, back- and front-view.

6, calyx with pistil.

7, side-view of fruit.

8, transverse section of fruit.

9, longitudinal section of fruit.

10, seeds.

11, embryo.

All enlarged, but in various degree.

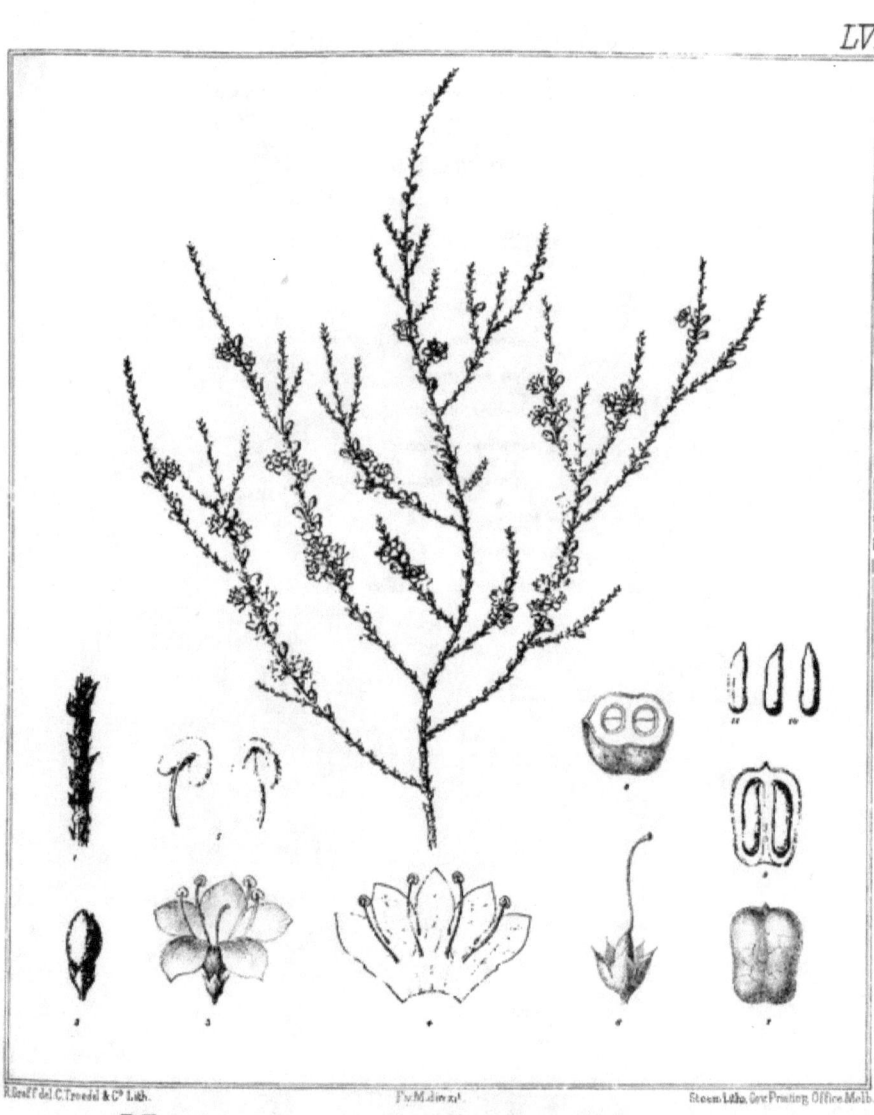

Myoporum salsoloides *Turczaninow.*

Myoporum Beckeri.

F. v. M. in Bentham's Flora Australiensis v. 7 (1870).

PLATE LVII.

Figure 1, unexpanded flower.

    2, expanded flower.

    3, corolla, laid open.

    4, stamens, front- and back-view.

    5, pistil.

    6 and 7, front- and side-views of fruit.

    8, transverse section of fruit.

    9, longitudinal section of fruit.

    10, seeds.

All enlarged, but in various degree.

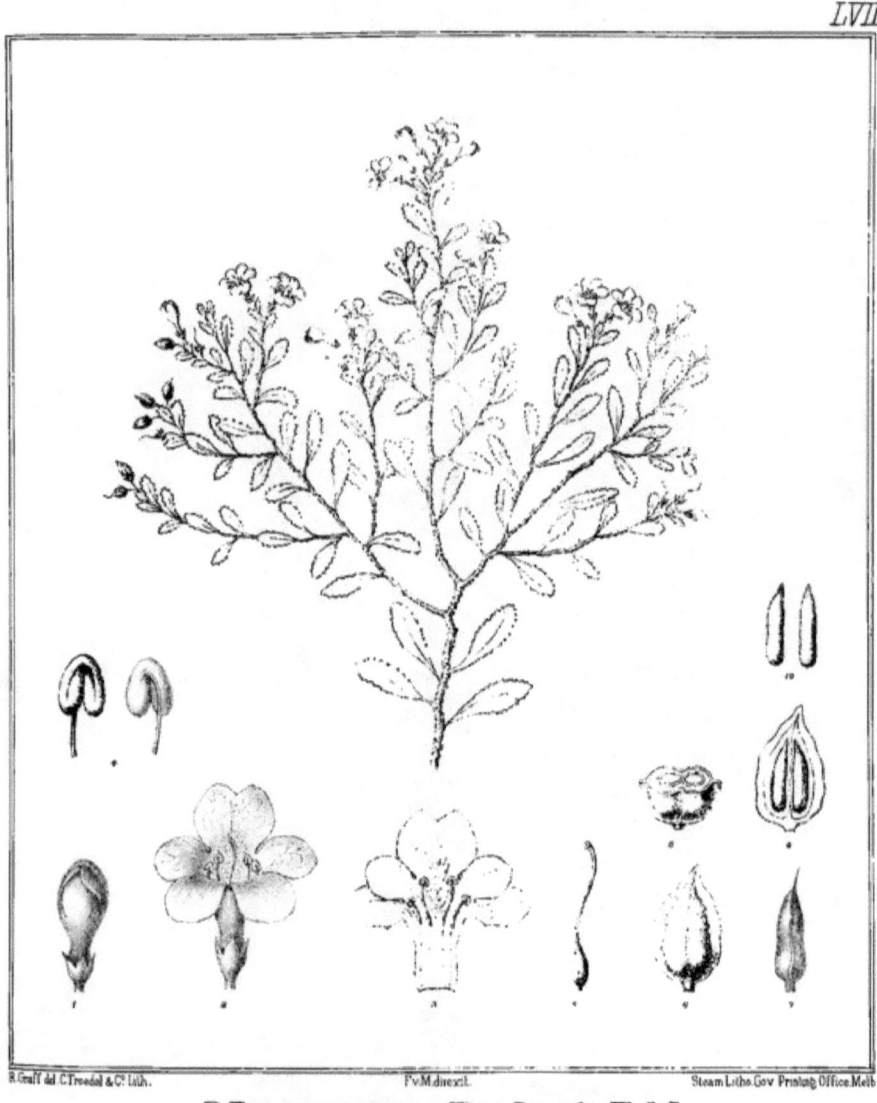

Myoporum Beckeri F.vM.

Myoporum floribundum.

A. Cunningham in Huegel enumeratio plantarum Novæ Holl. austro-occidentalis 78 (1837).

PLATE LVIII.

Figure 1, upper part of a leaf.
2, unexpanded flower.
3, expanded flower.
4, corolla, laid open.
5, stamens, front- and back-view.
6, calyx with pistil.
7, side-view of fruit.
8, fruit, seen from beneath.
9, transverse section of fruit.
10, longitudinal section of fruit.
11, seeds.

All more or less enlarged.

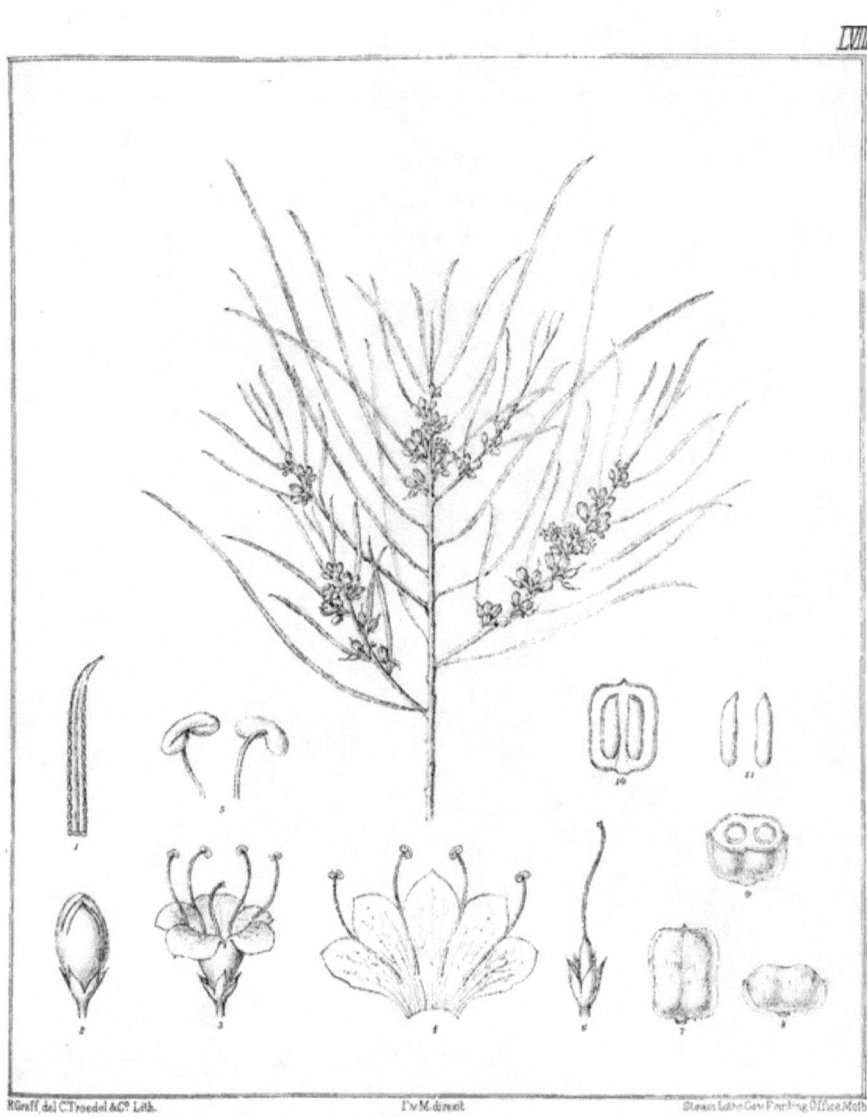

Myoporum floribundum. A.Cunningham.

Myoporum Bateæ.

F. v. M. in the Proceedings of the Linnean Society of New South Wales vi. 792 (1881).

PLATE LIX.

Figure 1, flower-bud.
2, unexpanded flower.
3, expanded flower.
4, corolla, laid open.
5, stamens, front- and back-view.
6, pistil.
7, side-view of fruit.
8, transverse section of fruit.
9, longitudinal section of fruit.
10, seeds.

All enlarged, but in various degree.

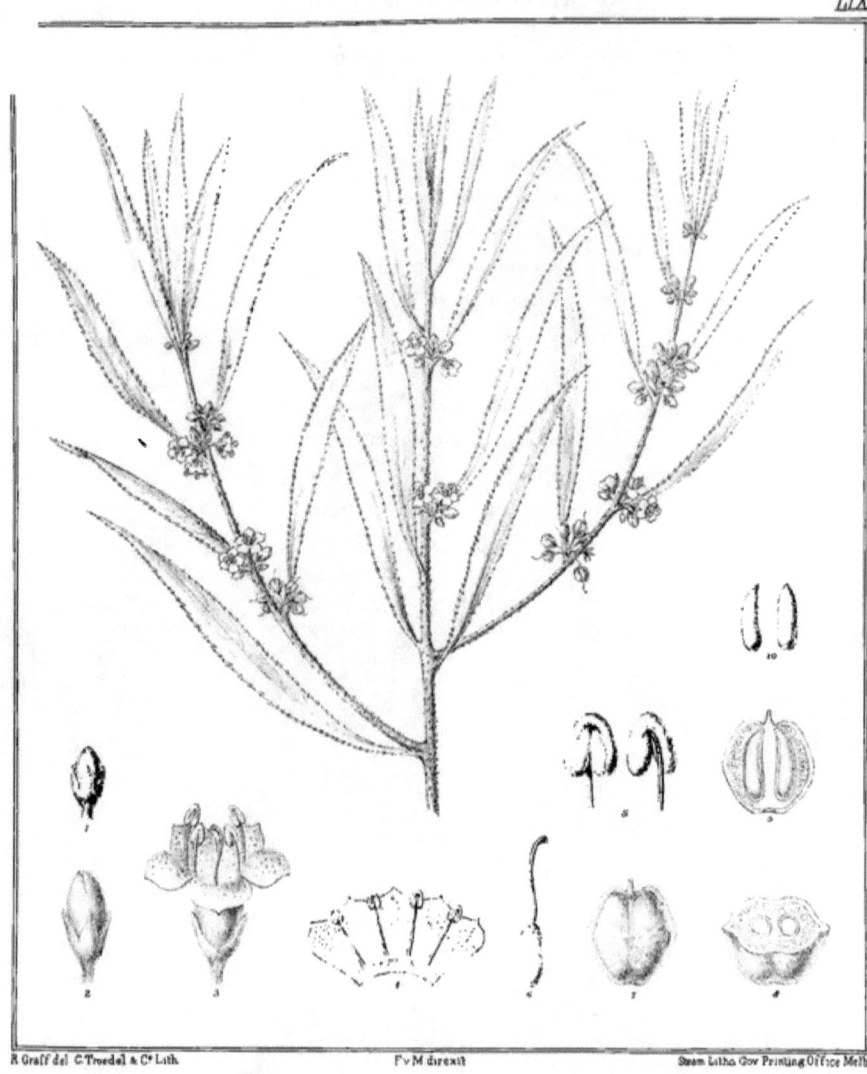

Myoporum Bateae FvM.

Myoporum platycarpum.

R. Brown, Prodromus floræ Novæ Hollandiæ 516 (1810).

PLATE LX.

Figure 1, portion of leaf.

2, unexpanded flower.

3, expanded flower.

4, corolla, laid open.

5, stamens, front- and back-view.

6, calyx with pistil.

7, fruit, side-view.

8 and 9, lower half of two fruits.

10, longitudinal section of fruit.

11, seeds.

All more or less enlarged.

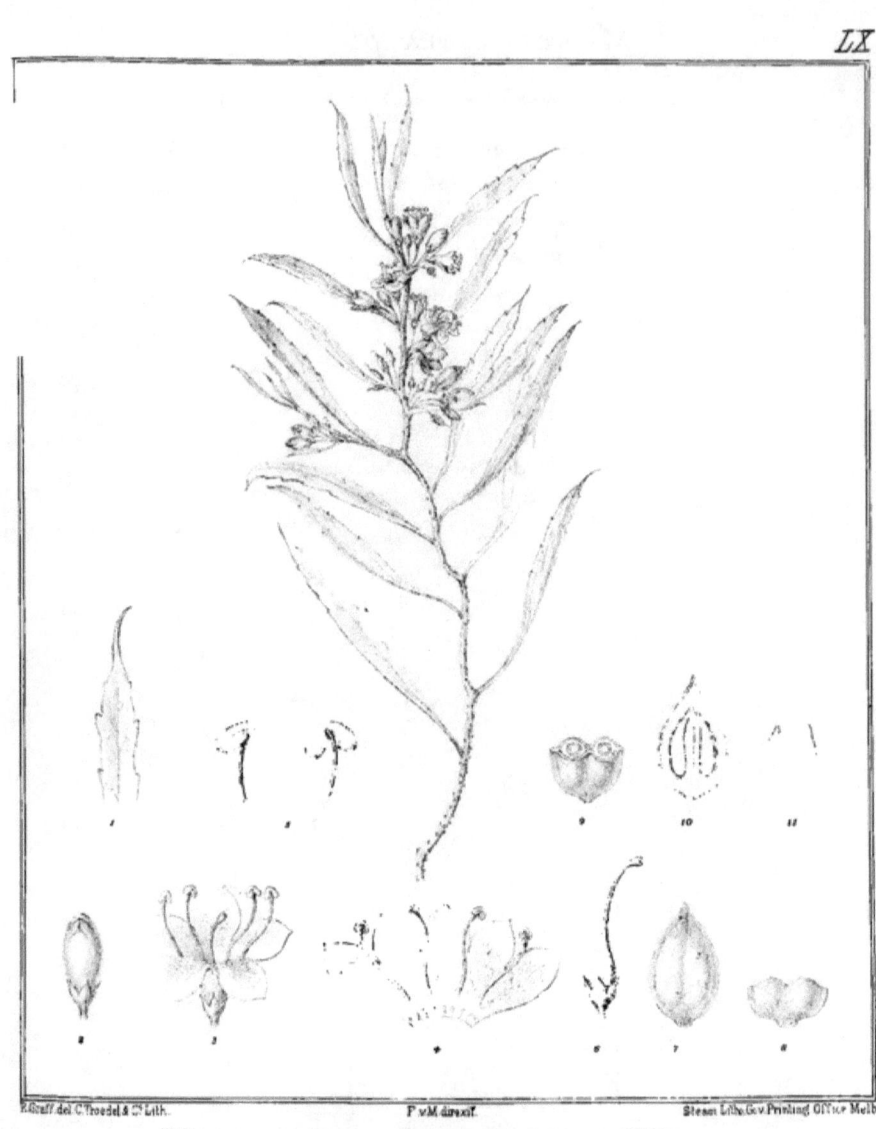

Myoporum platycarpum R.Brown.

Myoporum debile.

R. Brown, Prodromus floræ Novæ Hollandiæ 516 (1810).

PLATE LXI.

Figure 1, flower-bud.

2, expanded flower.

3, corolla, laid open.

4, stamens, front- and back-view.

5, calyx with pistil.

6, front-view of fruit.

7, transverse section of fruit.

8, longitudinal section of fruit.

9, seeds.

All enlarged, but in various degree.

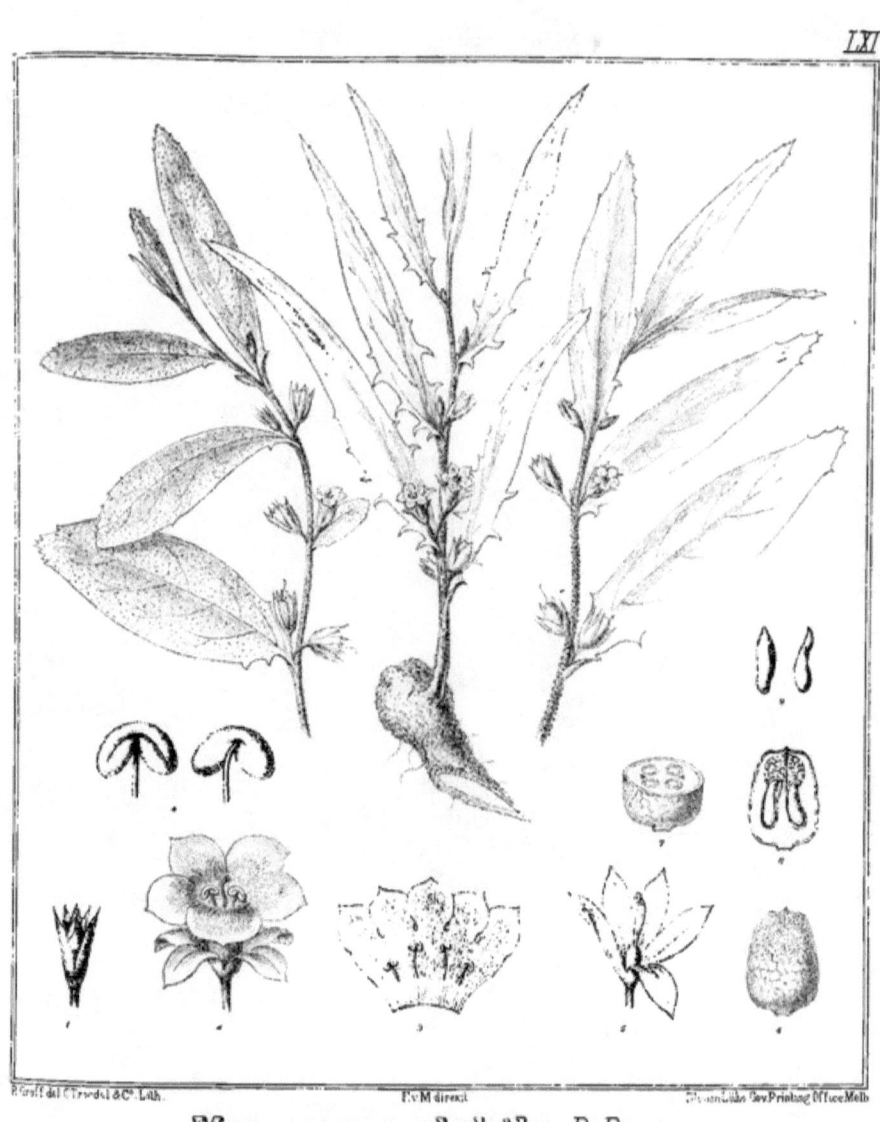

Myoporum debile R. Brown.

Myoporum humile.

R. Brown, Prodromus floræ Novæ Hollandiæ 516 (1810).

PLATE LXII.

Figure 1, unexpanded flower.

2, expanded flower.

3, corolla, laid open.

4, stamens, back- and front-view.

5, pistil.

6, side-view of fruit.

7, transverse section of fruit.

8, longitudinal section of fruit.

9, seeds.

All more or less enlarged.

Myoporum humile R.Brown.

Myoporum brevipes.

Bentham, Flora Australiensis v. 6 (1870).

PLATE LXIII.

Figure 1, leaf.

2, unexpanded flower.

3, expanded flower.

4, corolla, laid open.

5, stamens, front- and back-view, old and young.

6, pistil.

7, side-view of fruit.

8, transverse section of fruit.

9, longitudinal section of fruit.

10, seeds.

All enlarged, but in various degree.

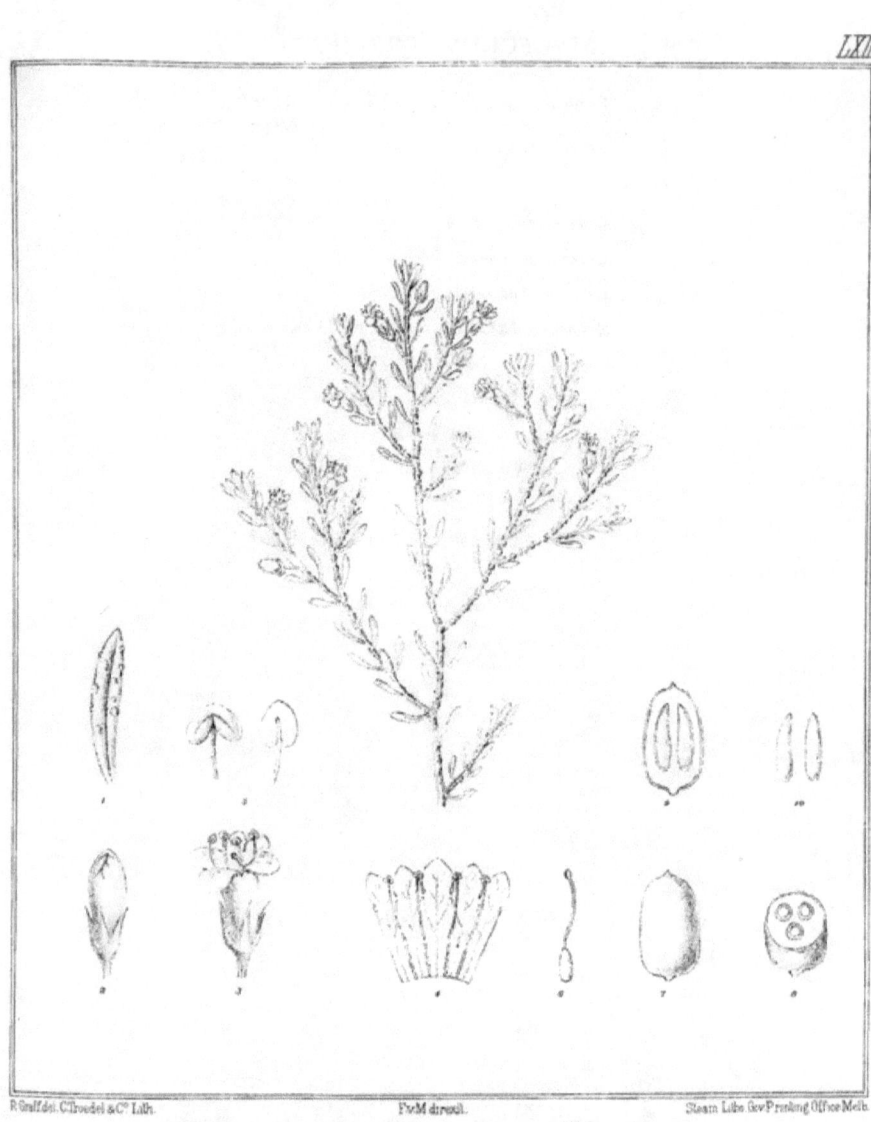

Myoporum brevipes BENTHAM.

Myoporum oppositifolium.

R. Brown, Prodromus floræ Novæ Hollandiæ 516 (1810).

PLATE LXIV.

Figure 1, unexpanded flower.

    2, expanded flower.

    3, corolla, laid open.

    4, stamens, front- and back-view.

    5, pistil.

    7, fruit, side-view.

    8, fruit, seen from near beneath.

    6 and 9, transverse section of two fruits.

    10, longitudinal section of fruit.

    11, seeds.

All enlarged, but in various degree.

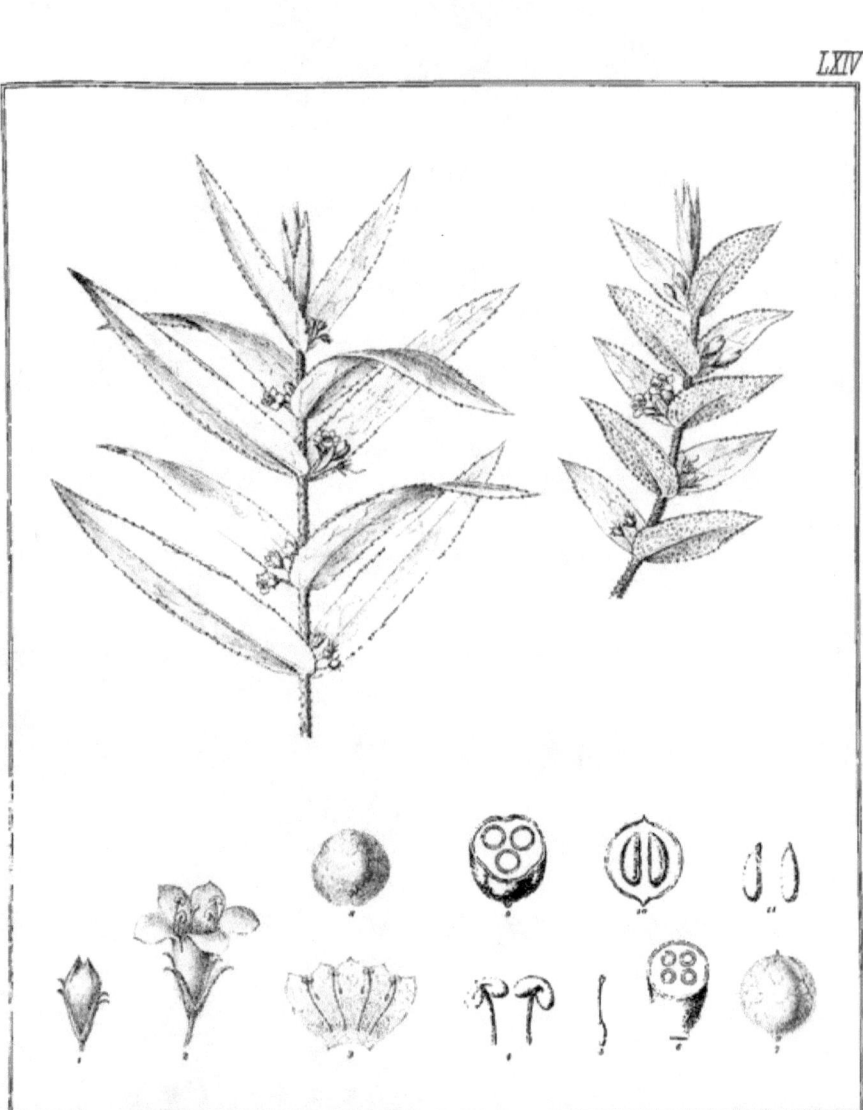

Myoporum oppositifolium R.Brown.

Myoporum serratum.

R. Brown, Prodromus floræ Novæ Hollandiæ 516 (1810).

PLATE LXV.

Figure 1, unexpanded flower.
    2, expanded flower.
    3, corolla, laid open.
    4, stamens, front- and back-view.
    5, calyx with pistil.
    6, side-view of fruit.
    7, fruit, seen from near beneath.
    8 and 9, transverse section of two fruits.
    10, longitudinal section of fruit.
    11, seeds.

All enlarged, but in various degree.

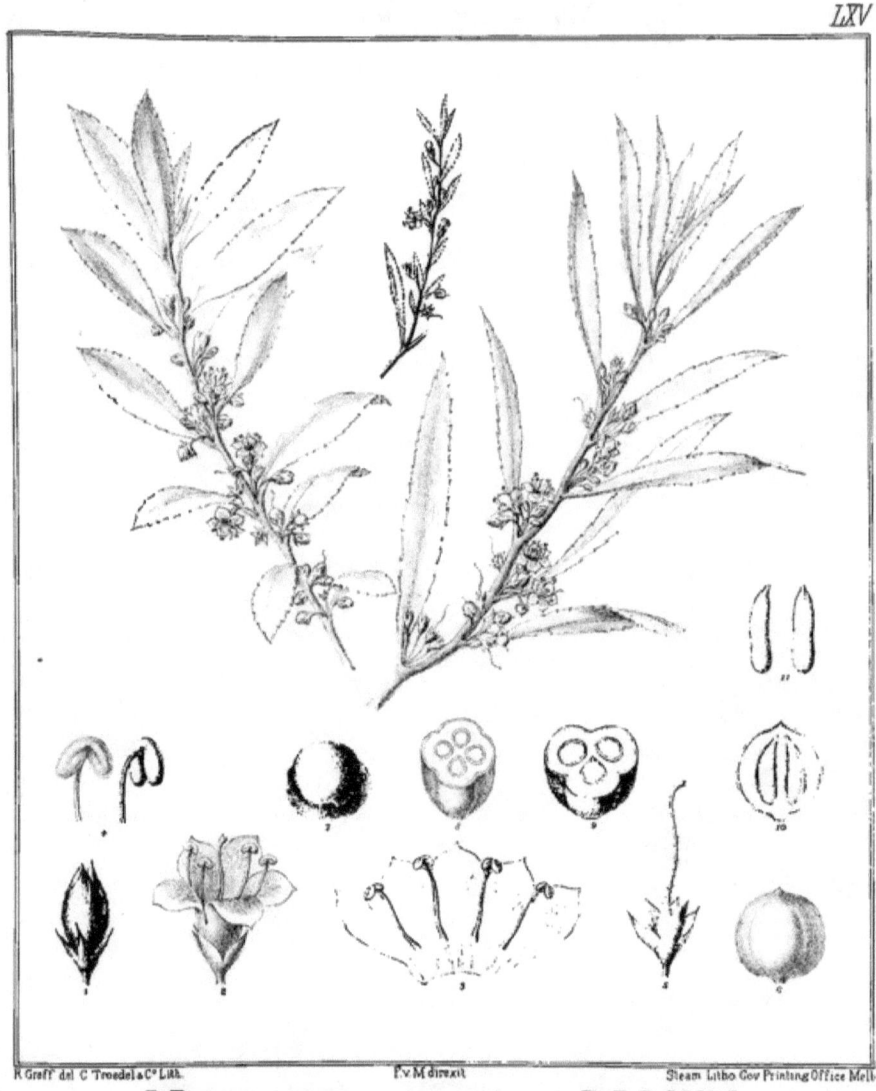

Myoporum serratum R. BROWN.

Myoporum viscosum.

R. Brown, Prodromus floræ Novæ Hollandiæ 516 (1810).

PLATE LXVI.

Figures 1, unexpanded flower.

2, expanded flower.

3, corolla, laid open.

4, stamens, front- and back-view.

5, calyx with pistil.

6, side-view of fruit.

7, fruit, seen from beneath.

8, transverse section of fruit.

9, longitudinal section of fruit.

10, seeds.

All more or less enlarged.

Myoporum viscosum R.Brown.

Myoporum laxiflorum.

Bentham in Flora Australiensis v. 6 (1870).

PLATE LXVII.

Figure 1, unexpanded flower.

2, expanded flower.

3, corolla, laid open.

4, stamens, front- and back-view.

5, pistil.

6, fruit with calyx.

7, fruit without the outer pericarp.

8, transverse section of fruit.

9, longitudinal section of fruit.

10, seeds.

All enlarged, but in various degree.

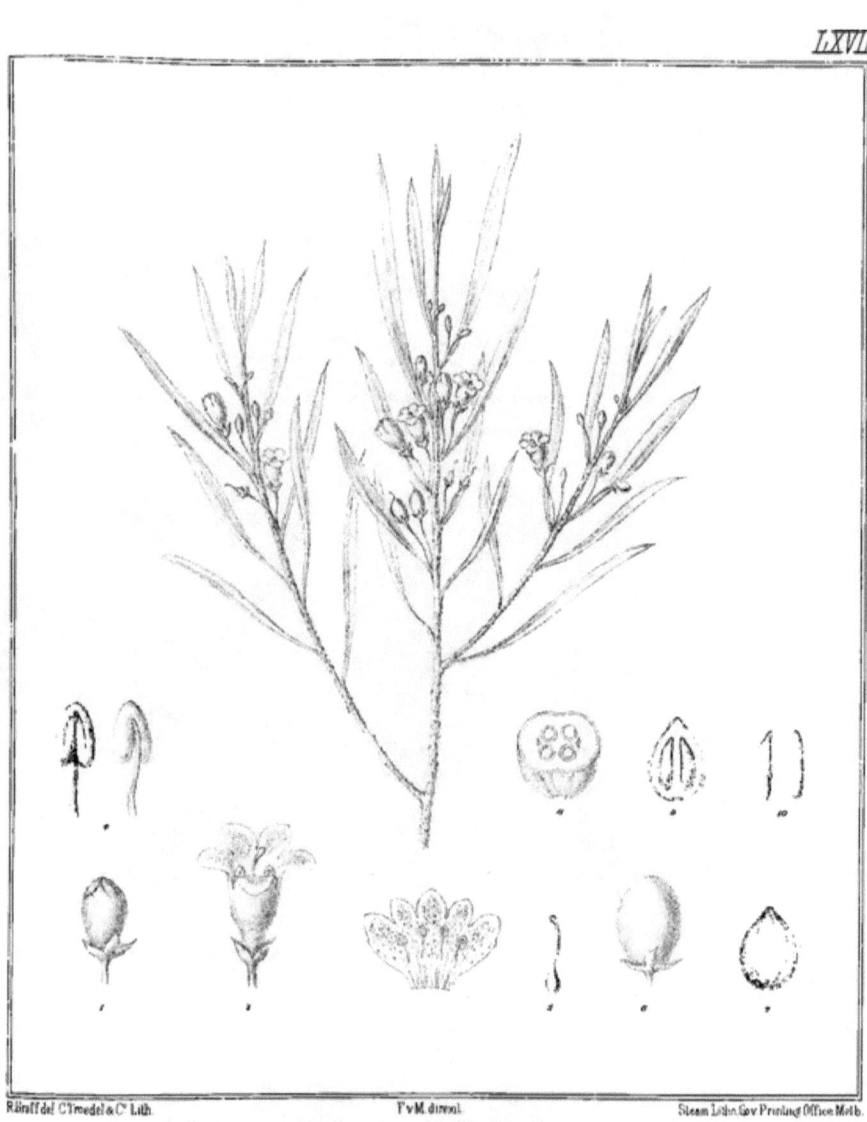

Myoporum laxiflorum BENTHAM.

Myoporum deserti.

A. Cunningham in Huegel's enumeratio plantarum 78 (1837).

PLATE LXVIII.

Figure 1, flower-bud.

    2, unexpanded flower.

    3, expanded flowers.

    4 and 5, two corollas, laid open.

    6 and 7, front- and back-view of stamens.

    8, calyx with pistil.

    9, fruit with calyx.

    10, fruit without the outer pericarp.

    11, transverse section of fruit.

    12, longitudinal section of fruit.

    13, seeds.

        All enlarged, but in various degree.

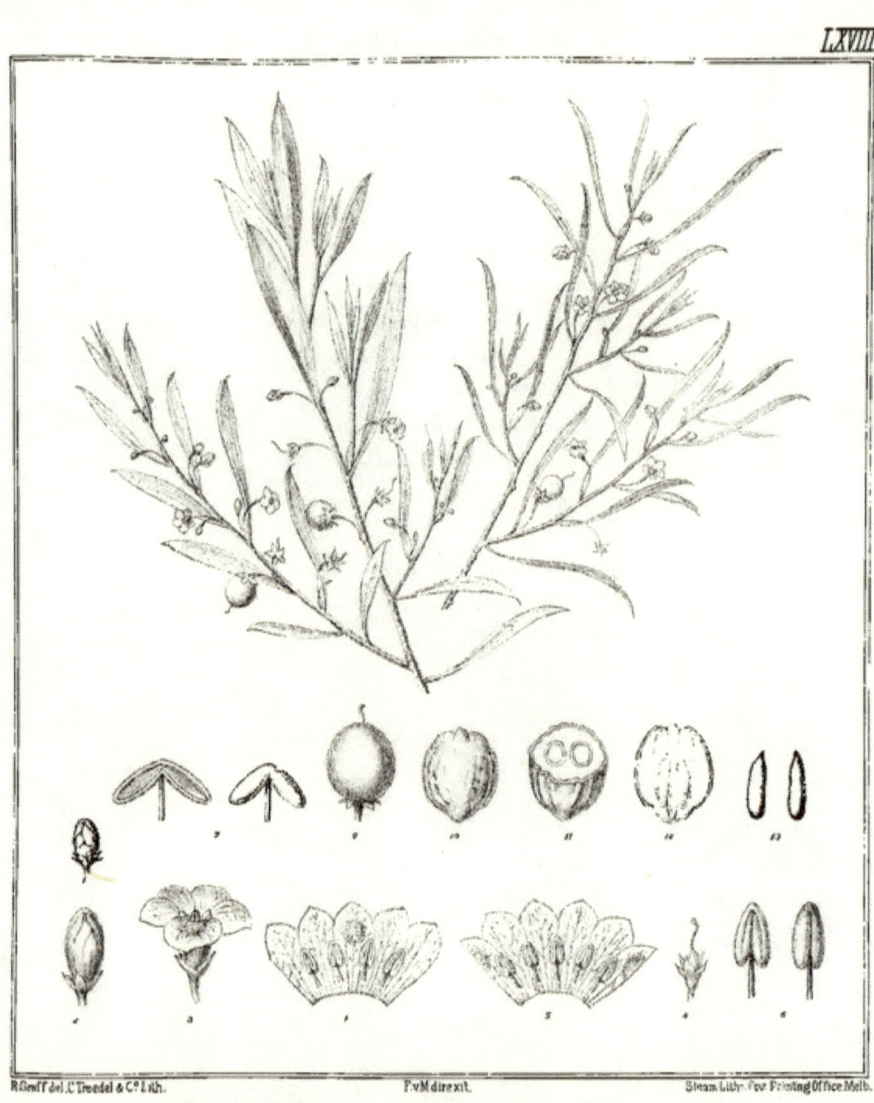

Myoporum deserti A. Cunningham.

Myoporum Dampieri.

Cunningham in A. de Candolle prodrom. syst. nat. regn. veg. xi. 708 (1847).

PLATE LXIX.

Figure 1, unexpanded flower.

2, expanded flower.

3 and 4, two corollas, laid open.

5, stamens, front- and back-view.

6, calyx with pistil.

7, fruit with calyx.

8, fruit without the outer pericarp.

9 and 10, transverse section of two fruits.

11, longitudinal section of fruit.

12, seeds.

All enlarged, but in various degree.

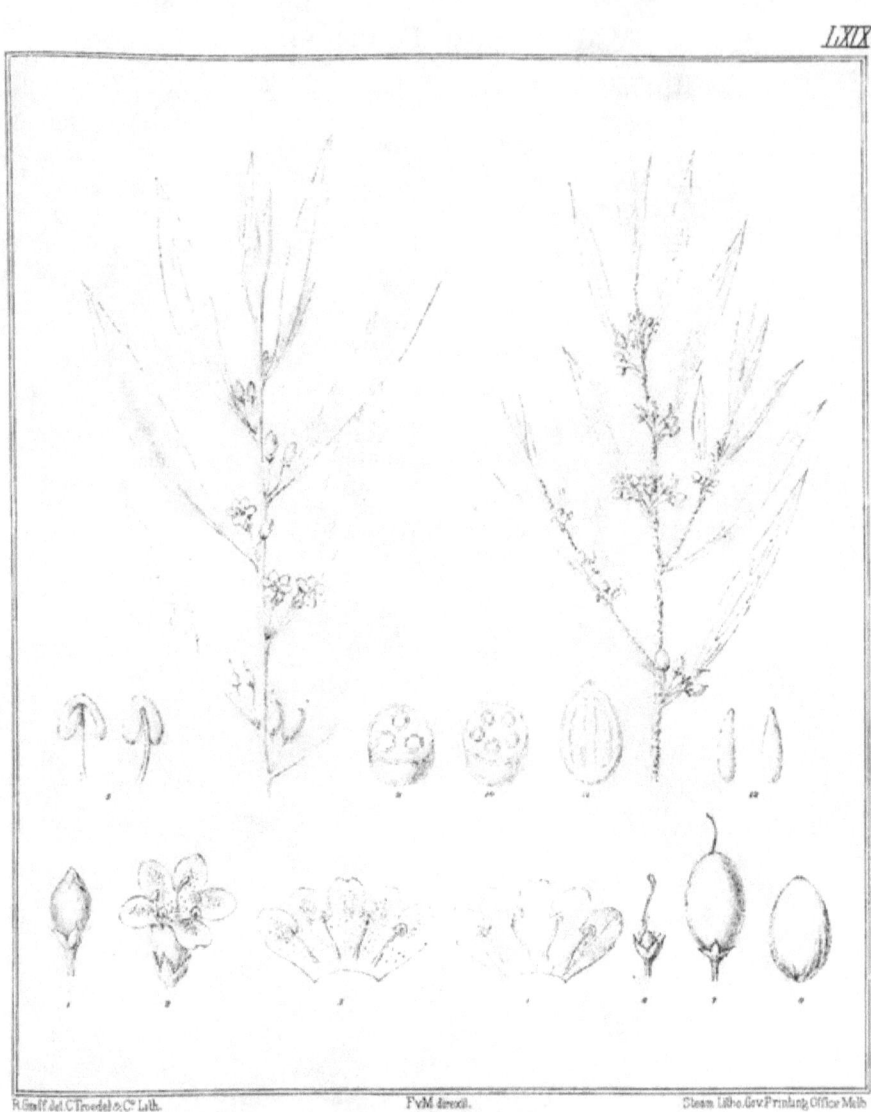

Myoporum Dampierii *Cunningham*.

Myoporum glabrum.

F. v. M. third supplement to systematic census of Australian plants 6 (1886).

PLATE LXX.

Figure 1, unexpanded flower.

2, expanded flower.

3, corolla, laid open.

4, stamens, front- and back-view, early and aged state.

5, pistil.

6, fruit with calyx.

7, fruit, the outer pericarp removed.

8, transverse section of fruit.

9, longitudinal section of fruit.

10, seeds.

All enlarged, but in various degree.

Myoporum glabrum FvM

Myoporum tenuifolium.

G. Forster, florulæ insularum Australium prodromus 44 (1786).

PLATE LXXI.

Figure 1, unexpanded flower.

2, expanded flower.

3, corolla, laid open.

4, stamens, front- and back-view, young and old.

5, pistil.

6, fruit with calyx.

7, fruit, the pericarp removed.

8, transverse section of fruit.

9, longitudinal section of fruit.

10, seeds.

All more or less enlarged.

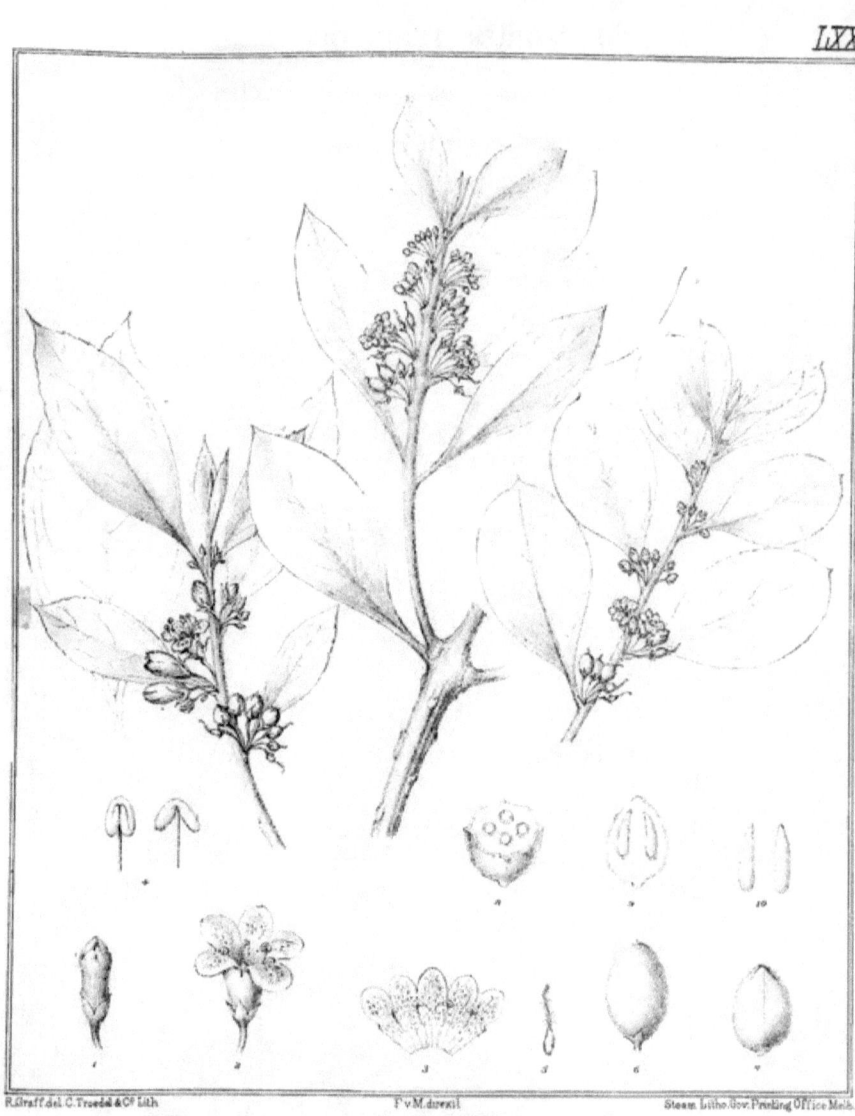

Myoporum tenuifolium FORSTER.

Myoporum insulare.

R. Brown, prodromus floræ Novæ Hollandiæ 515 (1810).

PLATE LXXII.

Figure 1, unexpanded flower.

    2, expanded flower.

    3, corolla, laid open.

    4, stamens, front- and back-view.

    5, pistil.

    6, side-view of fruit.

    7 and 8, transverse section of two fruits.

    9, longitudinal section of fruit.

    10, seeds.

        All more or less enlarged.

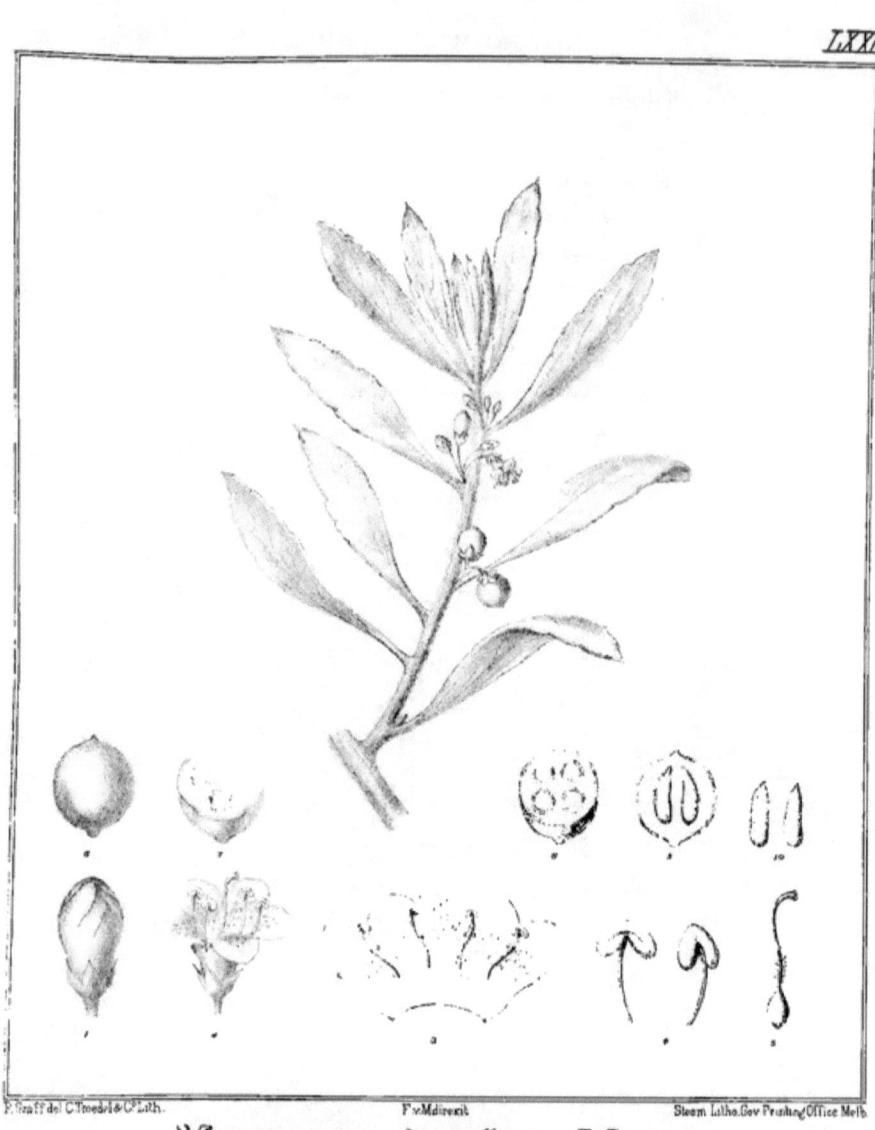

Myoporum insulare R. Brown.

Eremophila viscida.

Endlicher, novarum stirpium decades 51 (1839).

SUPPLEMENTAL PLATE I.

Figure 1, glandular hairs on corolla.

2, expanded flower.

3, corolla, laid open.

4, stamens, back- and front-view.

5, pistil.

6, fruit, viewed from the broad side.

7, fruit, seen from the narrow side.

8, transverse section of fruit.

9, longitudinal section of fruit.

10, seeds.

All more or less enlarged.

Supplemental plate I

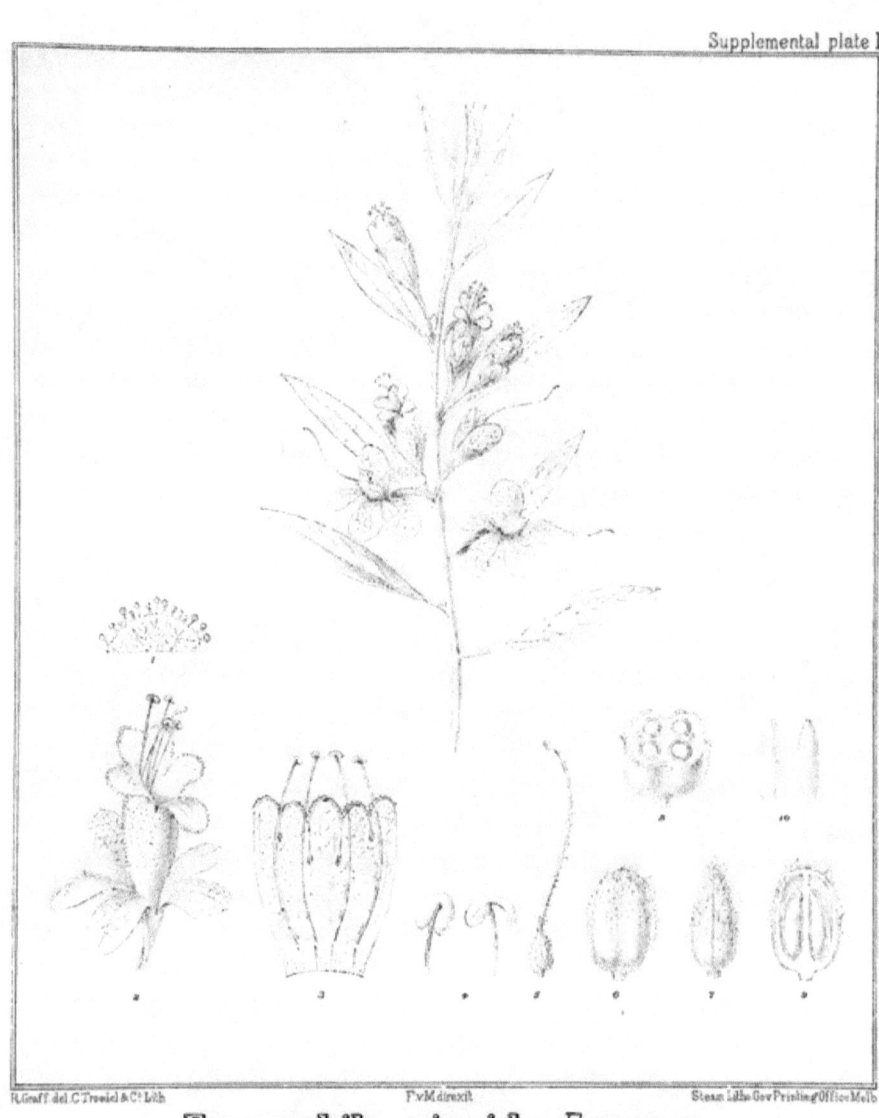

Eremophila viscida ENDLICHER.

Eremophila resinosa.

F. v. M. in Proceedings of the Royal Society of Tasmania iii. 296 (1858).

SUPPLEMENTAL PLATE II.

Figure 1, branched hairs on leaves and inflorescence.

    2, unexpanded flower.

    3, expanded flower.

    4, corolla, laid open.

    5, stamens, front- and back-view.

    6, calyx with pistil.

    7, side-view of fruit.

    8, transverse section of fruit.

    9, longitudinal section of fruit.

        All more or less enlarged.

Supplemental plate II

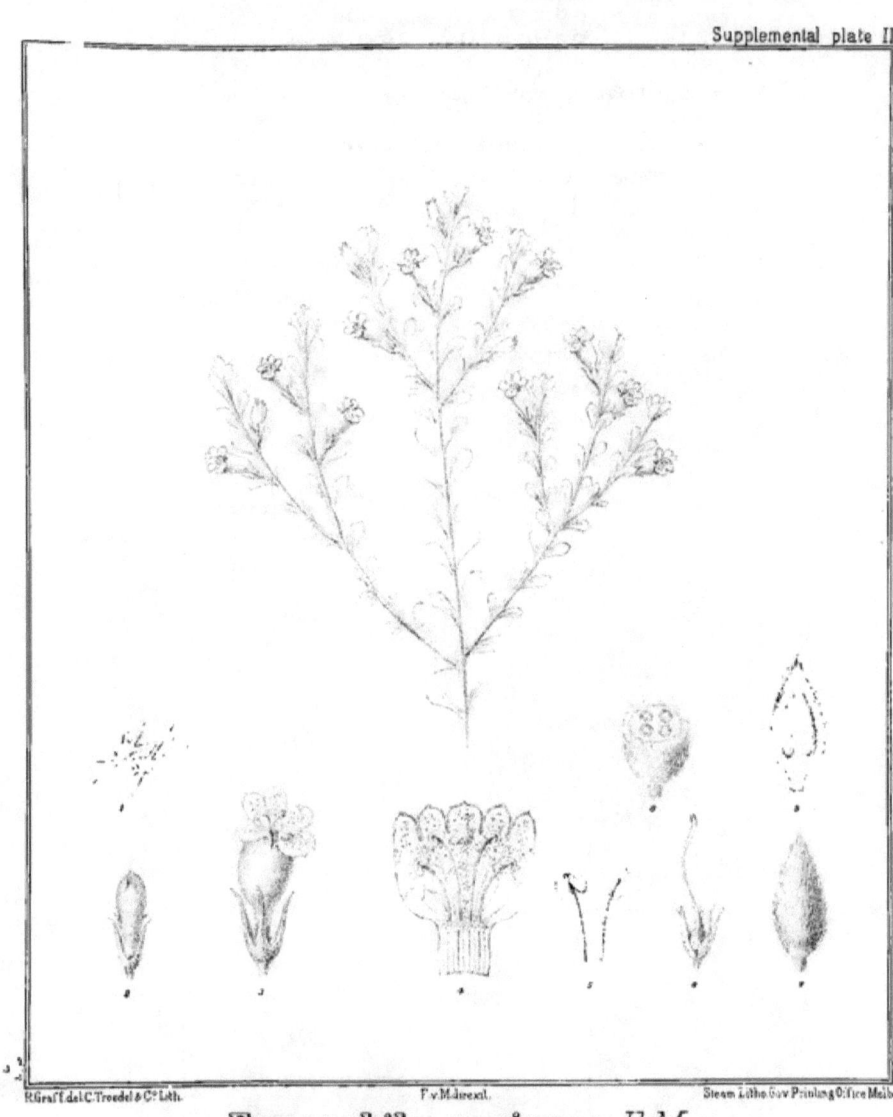

Eremophila resinosa *FvM.*

www.ingramcontent.com/pod-product-compliance
Lightning Source LLC
Chambersburg PA
CBHW032115230426
43672CB00009B/1740